THE

Secret World *of* Slugs *and* Snails

D1608190

THE

Secret World *of* Slugs *and* Snails

Life in the Very Slow Lane

DAVID GEORGE GORDON

SASQUATCH BOOKS
SEATTLE

Printed in the United States of America
Published by Sasquatch Books
Distributed by PGW/Perseus
15 14 13 12 11 10   9 8 7 6 5 4 3 2 1

Cover illustration: Karen Luke Fildes
Cover design: Rosebud Eustace
Interior design and composition: Anna Goldstein
Interior illustrations: Karen Luke Fildes

Library of Congress Cataloging-in-Publication Data

Gordon, David G. (David George).
  The secret world of slugs and snails : life in the very slow lane /
David George Gordon.
      p. cm.
  Includes bibliographical references.
  ISBN-13: 978-1-57061-611-2
  ISBN-10: 1-57061-611-6
  1. Gastropoda. I. Title.
  QL430.4G654 2010
  594.3—dc22

                            2010032929

Sasquatch Books
119 South Main Street, Suite 400
Seattle, WA 98104
(206) 467-4300
www.sasquatchbooks.com
custserv@sasquatchbooks.com

3 4015 07021 5874

To Jenni, Vea, and Julia

Contents

Foreword

by Ciscoe Morris

Let's face it: most folks, especially gardeners, despise slugs and snails. It's hard to appreciate slimy creatures that seem bent on gobbling up edible plants and prized ornamentals. I admit that I was among the ranks of slug and snail haters, until I read *The Secret World of Slugs and Snails*. Thanks to David George Gordon, I'm now so fascinated with these midnight marauders, I actually might even like them!

David George Gordon, a naturalist by education and training, is the perfect guide into the mysterious world of slugs and snails. In this fast and delightful read, you'll learn how these incredible creatures surf on slime, breathe, hitchhike to new places—and even think. You'll learn that the voracious plant-eating brown snail is none other than an escargot, introduced here by a French man in the 1800s (who, in my opinion, should have been taken out and shot for what he did!). You'll also learn about the ingenious ways slugs and snails defend themselves when under attack. There are slugs that can jettison their tail, slugs that can jump, and snails that give off a garlic odor that is effective at repelling hedgehogs and other predators (except maybe Italian ones). If all that doesn't hook you, wait until you read the steamy section on slug and snail love. Oh, la, la!

One thing that changed my opinion about slugs and snails was learning the amount of good they do. Their main role in nature is to eat and break down rotting organic substances, turning them into nutrients for plants. They're also a great food source for many mammals, reptiles, insects, and birds, and, of course, humans. Medically, they are proving useful too. Slug slime from our own Northwest native banana slug is being used with cancer drugs to make them much more effective in the fight to cure disease.

Despite all of their good qualities, there are still plenty of good reasons to do battle with slugs. For one thing, they have about 27,000 teeth, and they're good at using them. Slugs and snails eat several times their body weight every day. And, as the author points out, they're good at reproducing. In fact, when pickings get thin at the singles bar, the old adage "love thyself" takes on a whole new meaning with these critters. And don't think for a moment that you'll ever be able to eradicate these mollusk troublemakers from your garden. Studies quoted in this book found that removal of 17,000 slugs from a single garden in one year failed to make an appreciable dip in the slug/snail population. Fortunately David offers plenty of great suggestions on environmentally friendly, yet effective, ways to allow you to coexist with these remarkable creatures without sacrificing your favorite plants. David also includes a list of plants that slugs and snails tend to devour, and a list of ones to use as replacements that gastropods rarely, if ever, touch.

In truth, you'll never completely win the war against slugs and snails, but after reading David George Gordon's wonderful book and learning what incredibly fascinating creatures they are, you might not even care.

—Ciscoe Morris is the author of *Ask Ciscoe* and host of *Gardening with Ciscoe.*

Acknowledgments

This book would not be possible without the energies of several dozen friends, associates, and family members. I am deeply indebted to Barry Roth, who so freely shared his knowledge of all things malacological. I am grateful to Anne Depue, who advised and encouraged me at every stage of my literary journey up Mount Fuji. Likewise, I am thankful for Whitney Ricketts, a superb editor with boundless enthusiasm for the slimy subjects of this book, and for Kurt Stephan and Gary Luke of Sasquatch Books, who were helpful at every turn of the page. Thanks, also, to Anna Goldstein for her elegant book design. Last but not least, I thank my beloved wife, Karen Luke Fildes, for her unlimited patience and loving support of my work.

Common and Scientific Names of Land Slugs and Snails in this Book

(PRIMARY SOURCE: *Common and Scientific Names of Aquatic Invertebrates from the United States and Canada: Mollusks*, 2nd edition, American Fisheries Society.)

Ash-black gardenslug *Limax cineroniger*
Banana slug *Ariolimax columbianus*
Beaded lancetooth *Ancotrema sportella*
Blue-grey taildropper *Prophysaon coeruleum*
Brown gardensnail *Helix aspersa*
Brushfield hesperian *Vespericola pilosus*
Cellar glass-snail *Oxychilus cellarius*
Chocolate arion *Arion rufus*
Decollate snail *Rumina decollata*
Dromedary jumping-slug *Hemphillia dromedarius*
Earshell slug *Testacella haliotidea*
East African land snail *Achatina fulica*
Garlic glass-snail *Oxychilus alliarius*
Giant gardenslug *Limax maximus*
Giant Ghana tiger snail *Achatina achatina*
Greenhouse slug *Milax gagates*
Grey fieldslug *Deroceras reticulatum*
Grovesnail *Cepaea nemoralis*

Meadow fieldslug *Deroceras laeve*
Northwest hesperian *Vespericola columbianus*
One-ridge fieldslug *Deroceras monentolophus*
Oregon forestsnail *Allogona townsendiana*
Oregon lancetooth *Ancotrema hybridium*
Pacific sideband *Monadenia fidelis*
Pale jumping-slug *Hemphillia camelus*
Reticulate taildropper *Prophysaon andersoni*
Robust lancetooth *Haplotrema vancouverense*
Roman or escargot snail *Helix pomatia*
Scarletback taildropper *Prophysaon vanattae*
Warty jumping-slug *Hemphillia glandulosa*
West African land snail *Achachatina marginata*
Yellow slug *Limax flavus*
Yellow-bordered taildropper *Prophysaon foliolatum*

INTRODUCTION:

Why Slow and Steady Wins the Race

O Snail
Climb Mount Fuji,
But slowly, slowly!

—KOBASHI ISSA

Fast food, fast cars, fast relief from headaches and muscle pain—it appears that our species is obsessed with speed. Getting the job done quickly, whatever it may be, has become the mantra of many of us. We reach out for anything that will save us a few minutes, whether it's a fast-acting oven cleaner, a cup of coffee to go, an even higher-speed Internet connection, or a ride in the corporate Learjet.

And why shouldn't we want things to move as quickly as possible? After all, life is short, and anything that gives us more time to enjoy it is unquestionably an asset. Driving 65 miles per hour on the interstate will save several hours that might otherwise be wasted while traveling the same distance on a two-lane country road. So the choice for speed is clear—even if it means losing the opportunity to stop and smell the roses along the way.

Our love of speed is not solely linked to practicality. At its root is a seemingly innate appreciation for anything that moves faster than we can. Our heartbeats quicken at the sight of a galloping thoroughbred or the sound of a Formula One race car's roaring engine. We award Olympic medals to the fastest speed skaters, swimmers, and skiers, reinforcing the idea that the race belongs to the swift.

There are, however, other forms of life on our planet that don't necessarily feel this way. For these oft-overlooked creatures, it is slow and steady that wins the race—a notion proposed by Aesop more than 2,500 years ago. Although the tortoise gets the glory in Aesop's fabled contest with the hare, the story could just have easily gone to a slug or snail, two closely related organisms that, throughout their lives, refrain from doing anything that could even remotely be classified as speedy.

Snails move slowly, eat slowly, reproduce, grow, and die slowly. When threatened by a predator, they don't make a dash for the door. A land snail will slowly retract its body into the protective confines of its shell and wait for the invading bird, snake, beetle, or human to get bored and move on. This strategy may seem simplistic, but it works surprisingly well.

Slugs lead equally languid lifestyles. The current holder of the land speed record for slugs is the yellow slug (*Limax flavus*), a strapping 3–4-inch (7.5–10 cm) specimen from Eastern Europe. It clocks at peak speeds of 0.039 miles

(0.063 km) per hour. At this rate, the yellow slug could finish the 100-yard dash in a little under an hour and a half, assuming it didn't stop for snacks along the way. Incidentally, the Olympic champion for slowness among so-called "higher" life forms is the three-toed sloth, a generally torpid South American mammal that, at 0.15 miles (0.24 km) per hour, could rapidly outdistance the yellow slug in a similar competition.

The inability to outpace enemies has not lessened either the slug's or the snail's capacity for survival through the ages. Rather, both animals have existed comfortably, fairly unchanged from their ancestral prototypes, for hundreds of millions of years. Over that time, they've been forced to endure a succession of ice ages, earthquakes, volcanoes, and lesser climate events. Such conditions spelled doom for thousands of considerably larger, more biologically advanced, and significantly speedier species, including *Tyrannosaurus rex*, the woolly mammoth, and our hominid forebear, Neanderthal Man. In other words, the slug's and snail's slow-paced way of life has been time-tested, unlike our own rapid-paced bipedal approach, which began, geologically speaking, some mere 160,000 years ago.

By perseverance, the snail reached the Ark.

—C. H. SPURGEON, *Salt Cellars* (1889)

This seeming predisposition for life in the slow lane is just one way that slugs and snails lead lives vastly different from our own. Like all other members of the phylum Mollusca, slugs and snails are not blessed with any of the physical characteristics that we humans attribute to our species' success. First off, snails and slugs do not have big brains. In fact, like the Scarecrow in *The Wizard of Oz*, they lack them altogether. In place of a complex central processor with 100 billion interconnected nerve cells, a snail relies on its local control centers, called *ganglia*, to call the shots.

Second, slugs and snails do not have opposable thumbs. People are quick to point out that our thumbs give us the ability to make, grip, and use hand tools. Slugs and snails lack hands entirely—not to mention arms, legs, and toes. Yet they've found myriad ways to compensate for the dearth of corkscrews, electric drills, and other implements. Likewise, they've circumvented the need for a written or spoken language. Slugs and snails are capable of communicating with each other, but they do so through minute chemical clues contained in their silvery trails of slime.

Slugs and snails are cold-blooded creatures and, as such, do not reap the rewards of a reliable internal heat source like we warm-blooded organisms do. Neither of these mollusks has what we would consider a heart, and what passes for one is bathed in a pale blue fluid called *hemocyanin*, a copper-based protein that serves the same function as *hemoglobin*—the iron-based protein that carries oxygen to our bodies' cells and tinges our own blood bright red.

The alleged advantage of live birth? Forget that. The slugs and snails of our forests, fields, and gardens are egg-layers, depositing clutches of internally fertilized eggs protected by hard outer shells in nests beneath the leaf litter or first few inches of topsoil. Weeks or months later the eggs hatch, and the offspring are on their own. There's no parental involvement, no "bringing up baby" whatsoever—the hatchlings are fully equipped at birth to pursue identical paths to those of their parents. Speaking of which, many snails and slugs are *hermaphroditic*, meaning they are outfitted with both male and female reproductive systems (for a detailed discussion of this, see "Seven Wonders of Snaildom" later in this book). If no other options are available, such a snail or slug may be able to fertilize itself. Among humans, this feat is inconceivable—and offered as an option to others only as an insult. However, as many gardeners can attest, there's no shortage of land snails or slugs in nature, even without participation in the mammalian dating game.

What good are slow-going slugs and snails? This question implies that these creatures were created to serve humankind in some way. Fossil land snails taken from coal beds in America's Midwest, New Brunswick, and Nova Scotia indicate that they predate us by 260–350 million years. For this reason alone, it's preposterous to presume that such servitude could have been written into the grand scheme of things. "When we try to pick out anything by itself, we find it hitched to everything in the universe," observed the great American conservationist, John Muir. With this in mind, it might be more valuable to ask in what ways slugs and snails are "hitched" to us all.

Perhaps because of their physical and behavioral differences to us—or because most of our encounters with them involve disputes over grazing rights—people tend to overlook the many positive contributions of the native snail and slug species, perhaps not so much in our gardens, but certainly in the wild. In their natural settings, these unassuming invertebrates help disperse seeds and spores, break down decaying plant matter, and quite possibly keep other populations of small pests in check. Many are food for other invertebrates, as well as for amphibians, reptiles, birds, and mammals, including human beings.

Some snails are prized for their beautiful calcium-carbonate shells and others, including the charismatic East African land snail (*Achatina fulica*), have been invited into our homes as pets. They work their way into our folktales, feature films, and decorative motifs. Slugs and snails fill all these niches, providing ecological and cultural services without even once feeling the urge to step on the gas. Believe me, we would miss slugs and snails should we somehow eliminate them from our rapidly accelerating world.

An authority on West Coast land slugs and snails, Barry Roth, tells the story of a coworker who, early in his life, decided to abandon his path of religious study, leaving the seminary to become a student of *malacology*—the branch of biology that includes slugs and snails. Such a lifestyle change met with skepticism and a bit of hostility by the ex-seminarian's parents. "But why study snails, of all things?" they asked their son. Roth's coworker is said to have replied, "Slugs and snails are living reminders that not everyone gets to be an eagle."

Truly, there are important lessons to be learned from even the lowliest of land slugs and snails. More and more of us are seeing the wisdom of slowing down and succumbing to the quiet appeal of a more relaxed-pace approach to life's challenges. Global support for the slow food movement (which uses the land snail as its symbol) has inspired other "slow" subcultures, among them slow travel, slow shopping, and slow parenting. Each of these "slow" choices is fueled by the desire to lead intentional, moderate-speed existences with ample time for self-enrichment and internal growth.

"Ain't nobody slowing down no way; everybody's stepping on their accelerator," Mick Jagger howls in the Rolling Stones' song "Ventilator Blues." As we are seeing, survival of the fittest is not necessarily the same as survival of the fastest. Stuck in rush-hour traffic on a Los Angeles freeway, it's easy to recognize that, in the words of an anonymous sage, "the hurrier we go, the behinder we get."

> *The race is not to the swift or the battle to the strong, nor does food come to the wise or wealth to the brilliant or favor to the learned; but time and chance happen to them all.*
>
> —ECCLESIASTES 9:11

CHAPTER 1

Slug and Snail Basics

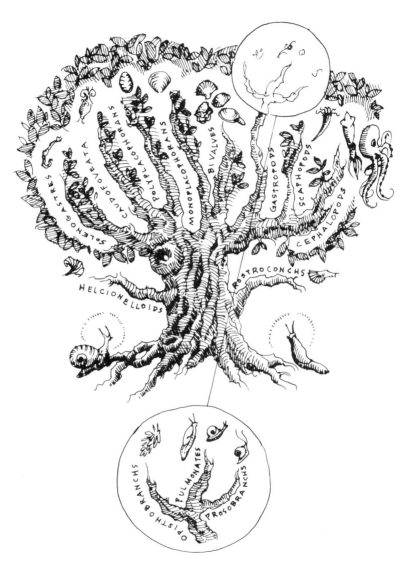

SOLENOGASTRES
CAUDOFOVEATA
POLYPLACOPHORANS
MONOPLACOPHORANS
BIVALVES
GASTROPODS
SCAPHOPODS
CEPHALOPODS
ROSTROCONCHS
HELCIONELLOIDS

OPISTHOBRANCHS
PULMONATES
PROSOBRANCHS

GASTROPOD FAMILY TREE

How ingenious an animal is a snail.
When it encounters a bad neighbor, it
takes up its house and moves away.

—PHILEMON (C. 300 BC)

Unlike warm-blooded humans, slugs and snails are cold-blooded organisms. Their bodies are boneless, lacking a backbone and spinal cord—conditions that put them in the collection of animals known as invertebrates. Ninety-five percent of all animate life on our planet, from nearly invisible roundworm parasites to 40-foot giant squids, falls into this category.

We vertebrates have divided the invertebrates among twelve smaller categories, or *phyla*, the largest of which (that is, the one with the most members) is the Arthropoda. This phylum of "joint-footed" animals contains a dizzying array of species—some 1,200,000 by most recent count—and includes common critters such as crabs and lobsters, scorpions, spiders, centipedes, millipedes, and insects. In terms of sheer numbers, the insects rule, with an estimated 350,000 species of beetle alone. That's more than 800 times the number of primate species, a statistic that inspired the British biologist J. B. S. Haldane to remark that "the Creator, if He exists, has an inordinate fondness for beetles."

Meet the Mollusks

The second largest invertebrate phylum, the Mollusca, is composed of so-called "soft-bodied" animals. Some 93,000 recognized species of living mollusks are scattered across every continent, including Antarctica. They occupy nearly every conceivable niche on earth. Mollusks have been found atop mountains and at the bottom of the sea,

DYAKIA STRIATA is the only land snail capable of true bioluminescence. But the function or functions of the bioluminescent glow of *D. striata* eggs and newly hatched snails is not known. Neither is the function of flashing in juveniles and most adults, according to J. J. Counsilman and P. P. Ong, whose study of these phenomena appeared in the *Journal of Ethology* in June 1988. Adults, juveniles, and eggs can be collected fairly easily in Singapore, where the snail with the eerie green glow was discovered in 1943.

in barren deserts and moist tropical rainforests, on wave-battered beaches and in the gently watered flowerbeds and vegetable patches of our own backyards.

Mollusks have soft, unsegmented bodies and a mantle—the organ that, in most species, secretes the materials for making the animal's solid outer shell. The shell is made of calcium carbonate crystals, and the blood of mollusks contains high concentrations of this salt in liquid form. The crystals are interspersed with organic materials, which give the shell added strength. *Conchology* is the study of mollusk shells, whereas *malacology* is the study of their makers. Like *oology* and *ornithology*, the separate studies of eggs and those that laid them, this distinction is clearly a product of the vertebrate mind.

See what a lovely shell,
Small and pure as pearl,
Lying close to my foot,
Frail, but a work divine,
Made so fairly well,
With delicate spire and whorl,
How exquisitely minute,
A miracle of design!

—ALFRED, LORD TENNYSON,
"The Shell," from *Maud* (1855)

Directly beneath the mantle is a fluid-filled chamber containing the internal organs of the respiratory, digestive, reproductive, and excretory systems. Most marine mollusks are what are known as broadcast spawners. When the time is right for making whoopee, they release eggs and sperm into the water column and let oceanic waves and currents bring the two together. The newly formed larvae from fertilized eggs usually go through a succession of anatomical and physiological changes, with each intermediate form more closely resembling that of their moms and dads.

INTERNAL ANATOMY

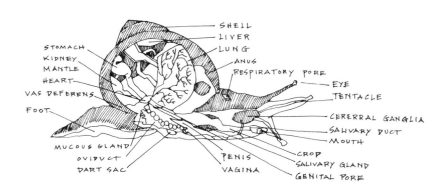

A snail's innards are well positioned to do what the animal does best, namely eating, breathing, and reproducing.

Other mollusks, especially those living on land, are hermaphroditic, possessing both male and female sex organs. While exempted from the war of the sexes, these animals have elaborate courtship and mating rituals that, in many instances, can end with mutual exchanges of genetic materials and produce two separate clutches of fertilized eggs.

The molluscan family tree branches into ten major lineages (or classes) of organisms, including two long-extinct lines. Many of the classes are familiar to most people—for instance, the oysters, scallops, mussels, and clams of Bivalvia, or the squids and octopuses of Cephalopoda. So, too, are those fascinating members of the Gastropoda, the slugs and snails. Lesser-known representatives include the fairly common but somewhat secretive seashore-dwellers known as chitons and the tusk shell, with their tubular, tooth-shaped outerwear, a highly prized trade good among Native American tribes. Even less familiar is the worm-like member of the class Caudofoveata, at home more than a mile down on the sea floor. Presumed to have become extinct 500 million years ago, living members of the limpet-like Monoplacophora were re-discovered in the 1950s, adding another branch to an already well-festooned tree.

The majority of modern mollusks are ocean-dwellers, comprising nearly a quarter of all recognized forms of life in the sea. Some are adapted to freshwater conditions, whether in rivers, lakes and ponds or, like the channeled apple snail (*Pomacea canaliculata*), in goldfish bowls and home aquaria. A few thousand species have figured out how to eke out a living on dry land. These silent but brave adventurers—the land-dwelling slugs and snails—are the subjects of this book.

> *When we consider this sluggish, and too often despised snail, without legs, fins, or wings, and yet performing the important function of locomotion with as much certainty and ease as animals more highly endowed, we cannot but admire the versatility of the Great Creative Mind in the various complete provisions made for the locomotion of all these humbler animals.*
>
> —EDWARD SYLVESTER MORSE,
> "The Land Shells of New England," from
> *American Naturalist* (1867–1868)

WHEN MOLLUSKS REIGNED

Judging by the abundance of mollusk fossils, the molluscan fauna of today represents just a fraction of the species that once inhabited the earth's ancient seas. For reasons still subject to debate, scads of these animals disappeared during what scientists call the Cretaceous-Tertiary extinction event, 65.5 million years ago.

Before this mass die-off, creatures such as the ammonite (which externally resembled the modern-day chambered nautilus) shared its ancient seas with a veritable freak show of molluscan forms, which included clams the size of Weber grills and curious cone-shaped reef-builders called rudists. These and other examples of early sea life may have been victims of rapidly changing ocean conditions, a collision of the earth with an enormous asteroid, or, possibly, both calamities occurring in rapid succession—a cosmic one-two knockout punch.

BIVALVE VS. GASTROPOD

Readers who'd rather not memorize multisyllabic scientific names will find relief in the fact that, of the aforementioned ten molluscan classes, most of the action, species-wise, is confined to only two—the Bivalvia and the Gastropoda.

Latin for "two-door," the name *bivalve* refers to the characteristic shell of these mollusks, which consists of two sections (called valves) made of calcium carbonate, joined at one edge by a flexible ligament hinge. Every bivalve wears one of these hard outer coverings, for protection both above and below the waterline. In nearly all instances, the bivalves can clasp their shell halves together, sealing in moisture and sealing out predators and foul weather. An odd exception is the geoduck clam (*Panopea generosa*), whose body is so plump that it cannot make its shell halves meet. Lucky for Tubby, the geoduck can burrow to a depth of three feet—far below the reach of all predators, with the exception of clam-digging humans.

A gastropod's shell consists of one, not two, sections, often with fancy markings and ornate projections. The name gastropod comes from the Greek *gaster*, meaning belly, and *podos*, meaning foot, which pretty much says it all. The gastropod slides along on its ventral surface (its "foot"), rhythmically contracting its foot muscles in waves to get around on land or in water. The majority of gastropods are adapted for aquatic conditions. They may withstand brief periods of exposure to the air during low tides, but, for most, that's as far as it goes. Like fish, these mollusks breathe through gills, taking in dissolved oxygen and releasing carbon dioxide gas though frilly apparati that resemble leaves or feathers.

Land snails used to live in the ocean, but moved ashore. Since nobody told them otherwise, they expected the land to be as wet as the water. We all make mistakes.

—WILL CUPPY, *How to Attract the Wombat* (1949)

A Trio of Gastropod Types

Many members of the gastropod group Opisthobranchia have unprotected gill clusters on their backs, hence these creatures' common name, the nudibranchs, or "naked gills." Sea-faring cousins of landlubber snails and slugs, they have unique strategies for protecting their fully exposed gills from hungry reef fishes. Nudibranchs feed on the tentacles of sea jellies and coral polyps, transferring the tentacles' still-active stinging cells (called *nematocysts*) to the tips of their gill filaments. This makes their gills as palatable as pasture thistles. Other opisthobranch species are shelled—proof that one can't make blanket statements about *anything* malacological.

N U D I B R A N C H

With their frilly gills and gaudy body colors, nudibranchs are often called "living flowers of the sea."

MOON SNAIL

Although it may look benign, the moon snail (Polinices lewisi) is an efficient predator, capable of drilling through shells of clams and oysters to eat the soft flesh within.

Marine representatives of the Prosobranchia include edible species such as the abalone, conch, and limpet, as well as the cones, volutes, and tritons, valued for their richly decorated shells. Although most marine snails are minute, a few can attain whopping proportions. The current size record holder rests in the collection of the Houston Museum of Natural Science: an Australian trumpet conch (*Syrinx aruanus*), measured at 31⅕ inches (80 cm) and 40 pounds (18 kg)—not bad for an animal without a backbone.

The Pond-snail . . . can creep with tolerable rapidity after the usual manner of snails, and has besides a curious method of progression without making any exertion of its own. In streams, when the animal has a mind to change its locality without needing to exert itself, it achieves the task of converting the journey into a voyage, and foot into a boat. This transformation is soon effected, the animal first crawling up some plant that projects out of the water, reversing its position, so that the shell lies undermost, and then hollowing the foot so as to form into a shallow boat-like shape. It then looses its hold on the supporting plant, and boldly launches itself on the surface."

—THE REVEREND J. G. WOOD, M.A., F.L.S.,
The Illustrated Natural History (1863)

FLORIDA APPLE SNAIL

Many pond snail species lay their eggs out of water on emergent vegetation, thus preventing their progeny from being eaten by fish.

With the exception of a few genera of snails and slugs from moist tropical climes, all land-dwelling gastropods belong to the order Pulmonata, the "lunged" land snails and slugs. These creatures inhale atmospheric oxygen and exhale carbon dioxide, just like we do while breathing. For the land snail and slug, this activity involves only one lung, not two. A small pore, called a *pneumostome*, opens and closes with each breath, its aperture widening and narrowing accordingly. Watch closely as a slug slides across your garden path, and you may spy this small, circular opening on the right side of its body (on a land snail, this anatomical feature is partially, if not wholly, concealed by the shell). Move even closer on a cold morning and you might see a wisp of moist air—"slug breath"—as the animal releases an exhalatory gasp. Considerably less complex than a bird's, reptile's, or mammal's paired lungs, the breathing apparatus of pulmonate snails or slugs is a far cry from a simple sac. Both in its cellular makeup and overall function, this highly vascularized organ is on par with the lung of an adult newt or salamander.

LOOK MA, NO OPERCULUM!

The shell of a pulmonate snail is devoid of an *operculum* (a Latin term that, literally translated, means "little lid"). "Too bad," one might presume. When danger comes calling, a marine snail can shut the front door, an oval-shaped sheet of hornlike protein, to effectively block the opening to its shell. Land snails must make do without such protection. Instead, they may seal off the shell's opening with what amounts to a weatherproof skin, called an *epiphragm*, made of calcium carbonate—the same material as the snail's shell—mixed with mucus.

The ubiquitous brown gardensnail (*Helix aspersa*) is one such epiphragm-maker. As winter approaches, it withdraws into its shell, folding its foot lengthwise, then pulling in the head, followed by the posterior, or "tail" end. It then secretes this thin skin which, when dry, is strong enough to deflect attacks by tiger beetles and other snail-eaters. The epiphragm is sufficiently porous to admit oxygen and vent any waste gases from respiration. It is also simultaneously waterproof and water-permissive: while keeping out rainwater and snowmelt, the epiphragm "breathes" slightly, maintaining the interior humidity at a comfortable level for the hibernating snail.

SNAIL-SICLES ANYONE?

Studies have shown that an epiphragm affords its maker a degree of protection against the extreme cold of winter. But even more important, the snail's body cells have the special gift of tolerating sub-zero temperatures for a limited time. In one set of lab experiments, batches of *Helix aspersa* were subjected to conditions at which the snails' body fluids would spontaneously freeze, literally forming ice crystals in the snails' bodies. Defrosted, the snails showed no signs of cold-induced damage.

Nice trick, eh? Some species of worms, amphibians, and fish rely on organic forms of "antifreeze" in their bloodstreams and bodies to keep them frost-free. However, if the lab snails had similar chemical defenses, they kept them well hidden. To date, scientists are unclear about how these creatures have acquired their remarkable cold-hardiness.

There for five or six months he sleeps, free from the pangs of hunger and the blasts of winter, and when the balmy breezes of spring blow up from the south, he breaks down and devours the protective membrane and goes forth with his home on his back to seek fresh leaves for food and to find for himself a mate.

—W. S. BLATCHLEY,
Gleanings from Nature (c. 1899)

16

SNAILS WITHOUT SHELLS

Several pulmonate species come equipped with shells that are too small to house their slug-like bodies effectively. Evolutionary intermediates between land snails and land slugs, these oddities are called semi-slugs. Another group of pulmonates lack shells altogether or sport tiny, cap-like rudimentary shells, in some instances concealed within the animal's skin. It is this group of pulmonates that scientists call the true slugs—in other words, the shell-less snails.

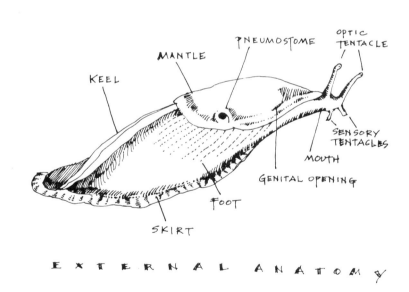

EXTERNAL ANATOMY

Slugs and snails share the basic body parts that have served them well for millions and millions of years.

Marine, freshwater, and land snails need rich sources of calcium to construct their shells. Freed from the burden of shell building, slugs can successfully occupy a broader range of habitats, including those with volcanic, calcium-poor soils. There's a significant trade-off, though: slugs are more prone than snails to desiccation, and therefore are more dependent on moisture to survive. Wherever there is volcanic activity, wet weather conditions, and plenty of plant life on which to feed (for example, on the island of Borneo or throughout the Pacific Northwest), the odds are best for finding slugs in abundance.

Traditionally the relationships among the various genera and species of gastropods were reckoned on the basis of shared traits, including the form and placement of gills, genitalia, and other anatomical features. Modern DNA analysis has given taxonomists reason to revisit the traditional classificatory scheme, first proposed by Swedish taxonomist Carl Linnaeus in 1735 and modified, enhanced, and embellished many times since then. Comparing the chromosomal makeup of pulmonate species is confirming what many malacologists had suspected for some time—that land snails and slugs have evolved from several different ancestral stocks, creating numerous lineages, some more distinct than others, filled with the progeny of convergent, divergent, and parallel evolution.

Slug and Snail Speciation

More than 2,000 species of pulmonate mollusks exist worldwide. Like other forms of invertebrate life, they run the gamut of sizes and shapes. Some, like the East African land snail, are quite massive, wearing whorled brown shells, 11 inches (28 cm) or more in diameter. According to the *Guinness Book of World Records*, the largest land snail on record was a giant Ghana tiger snail (*Achatina achatina*) collected in the African nation of Sierra Leone in 1976. Named "Gee Geronimo" by its owner, Christopher Hudson of East Sussex, England, this mega-mollusk measured 15½ inches (39⅓ cm) from head to tail and weighed a tad more than 2 pounds (900 g).

Many other land snails and slugs are miniscule. Arguably among the smallest of land snails, the *Truncatellina claustralis* of northern Europe can stuff itself into a tightly twisted shell less than ⅟₂₀ of an inch (1.5 mm) in length. Worldwide, about half of all land snail species and almost 90 percent of all individual snails are less then ⅕ of an inch (5 mm)—about the size of the bearded chin on a Lincoln-head penny. Members of the micro-snail family Pupillidae account for almost 10 percent of the entire North American pulmonates fauna. At some sites, they comprise more than a third of both the total number of species and of individuals. In some places, the number

19

of pupillid land snails can exceed 5,000 individuals per square meter.

The *Checklist of the Land Snails and Slugs of California* by Barry Roth and Patricia S. Sadeghian reports that 284 species and 110 subspecies live in the Golden Bear State. Robert G. Forsyth's *Land Snails of British Columbia* lists 92 species of terrestrial mollusks, native and introduced to this province. Many of these species are widespread, with established places of residence on both sides of the U.S.–Canada border.

> *One of the land slugs,* Limax noctiluca, *emits light; and the eggs of another,* Arion, *have been noticed to be luminous for nearly two weeks after being deposited.*

> —CHARLES FREDRICK HOLDER,
> *Half Hours With the Lower Animals* (c. 1905)

Gastropods Galore

The Olympic Peninsula—a wet, heavily forested, and largely undeveloped portion of Washington State—is a treasure trove for gastropod hunters. By conservative counts, more than seventy gastropod species currently

A SEARCH OF FORTY NURSERIES, botanical gardens, and other plant-based facilities on six of the Hawaiian Islands uncovered twenty-nine non-native snail and slug species, including some that had never been reported in Hawaii before. Most of these unwanted species had first arrived in Oahu, then spread to the other islands, concluded the searchers—a research team from the University of Hawaii at Manoa.

occupy this fertile ground. Among these seventy are fifty-six different species of land snails and slugs. "These numbers include three or more endemic slugs and two or more endemic snails," according to Branley A. Branson, author of the scientific paper "Freshwater and Terrestrial Mollusca of the Olympic Peninsula, Washington." He adds, "Such endemics, however, are only one of four molluscan elements present on the Olympic Peninsula. The remaining three elements are comprised by pre-glacial relicts, by re-invaders from the south, and by exotic species introduced by folly of humans."

INTRODUCED SPECIES

Whether through human folly or sheer neglect, non-native land snails and slugs have been distributed throughout

North America, in some instances, at the expense of native species. By leaving their natural predators and sources of parasites behind, introduced species can often flourish in their new worlds, outcompeting the native gastropods and sometimes, as is the case with one Mediterranean species, the decollate snail (*Rumina decollata*), actively feeding on them.

For the most part, the slugs and snails encountered in flower and vegetable gardens, hedgerows, and other human-constructed habitats are non-native, unintentionally introduced species. We unwittingly create ideal residences for these species, with ample food and water and, often, the near-complete absence of predators. Methods for ridding one's property of these uninvited guests are presented in the "Sharing Our Gardens" chapter later in this book.

A FEW WELCOME EXOTICS

The spread of exotic pulmonates was greatly assisted by the once-common practice of transporting plant materials, often infested with slugs, land snails, and other invertebrate hitchhikers, in the cargo holds of tall ships. Gardeners may be surprised to learn that the ubiquitous night crawler worm (*Lumbricus terrestris*) was brought to North America from Europe in much the same way, perhaps in potted plants aboard the *Mayflower* and other early colonists' vessels. It's not unusual, though, for people to intentionally introduce non-native mollusks to foreign lands. Most of the oysters now cultivated on our nation's Pacific Ocean coast are of Japanese origin, brought here as "seed"—tiny larvae attached to chips of oyster shell—in the 1920s, '30s, and '40s. Likewise, the Mediterranean mussel (*Mytilus galloprovencialis*), a European species, is often grown side-by-side with the native bay mussel (*Mytilus edulis*) on West Coast shellfish farms. It's likely that the exotic brown gardensnail and, possibly, its relative, the Roman or escargot snail (*Helix pomatia*), were released here by similarly ambitious mollusk farmers.

Pros and Cons of Living with Pulmonates

Humankind's relationship with land snails and slugs has been both bothersome and beneficial. As agricultural pests, the pulmonates are among the few animals on our planet that directly compete with people for food supplies. Their depredations on crops such as beans, celery, citrus fruits, and commercially grown edible mushrooms can cause many millions of dollars in damage annually. It's been estimated that in some years, the chocolate arion (*Arion rufus*), a well-established non-native species, has munched its way through more than 75 percent of Washington's strawberry crop.

> *The writer collected over two thousand specimens [of the yellow slug,* **Limax flavus**] *in 1884 in the heart of the city of Washington, not far from the Smithsonian Institution, in whose collections more than a thousand were placed.*

> —RICHARD ELLSWORTH CALL,
> *A Descriptive Illustrated Catalogue of the Mollusca of Indiana* (c. 1898)

EAST AFRICAN LAND SNAIL

Once sold as pets and kept in classrooms, giant African land snails can wreak havoc on local flora and fauna if released from captivity.

Land slugs and snails have also been indicted as carriers of *Salmonella* bacteria and other diseases. Many species serve as intermediate hosts for parasites, and cattle, sheep, deer, poultry, and other animals that eat them can become ill and eventually die from the experience. Avid gardeners and land-snail collectors may want to wash their hands thoroughly after reading this section.

On the positive side, the pulmonates perform many valuable functions. In their non-garden settings, they help disperse seeds and spores, break down decaying plant and animal matter, and, as natural recyclers, return nutrients to the forest food web through their nitrogen-rich feces. Some scholars have suggested that, by grazing on the grasses and other plants that might otherwise overshadow redwood tree seedlings, California's giant-sized banana slug (*Ariolimax columbianus*) directly shapes the growth of its preferred habitat.

SNAILS AS HEALERS: SNAIL-WATER

Throughout history, land snails have been credited with curative powers. Eighteenth century pharmacists believed that certain ingredients in snail flesh could ward off consumption (we now call this lethal disease tuberculosis), for which an effective antibiotic had yet to be devised. Among the remedies in *Pharmacopoeia Pauperum*, a collection of medicines in use by London hospitals in the early 1700s, is the following recipe for snail-water:

> *Take Garden-Snails cleansed and bruised 6 Gallons,*
>
> *Earthworms washed and bruised 3 Gallons,*
>
> *Of common Wormwood, Ground-Ivy, and Carduus, each one Pound and half,*
>
> *Penniroyal, Juniper-berries, Fennelseeds, Aniseeds, each half a Pound,*
>
> *Cloves and Cubebs bruised, each 3 Ounces,*
>
> *Spirit of Wine and Spring-water, of each 8 Gallons.*
>
> *Digest them together for the space of 24 Hours,*
>
> *And then draw it off in a common Alembick.*

Nearly 300 years later, a team of South Korean scientists demonstrated that acharan sulfate, a compound in the tissues of the East African land snail, was an effective tumor-suppressant, decreasing the weight and volume of murine Lewis lung tumors in mice by 40 percent. Other health care researchers have gained insights into the human nervous system by studying the East African land snail's super-sized neurons.

CULINARY DELIGHTS: LAND SNAIL PIE

The West African land snail (*Achachatina marginata*) is but one of several dozen land snail species eaten by humans. Studies have suggested that this easily collected animal is more protein-rich than beef, and considerably more cost-effective. In addition to protein, the raw meat of this animal and its kin contains iron, calcium, magnesium, phosphorous, copper, selenium, zinc, and vitamins

IN THE NOW-CLASSIC *Why Not Eat Insects?* (1883), British social reformer Vincent M. Holt told his countrymen that lower classes could easily sustain themselves on insects and other overlooked but abundant resources. "Masters might prepare savory snail dishes, according to the recipes used in all parts of the Continent," Holt suggested, adding that, "in a course of time, the servants would follow suit." To help others practice what he preached, Holt included two sample menus at the end of his book, both of which began with a soup course of *Potage aux Limacons*. He also championed slugs as wholesome foodstuffs for all, suggesting that "the most palatable dishes" could be made from common species of gardenslugs, and that the larger ones "might be treated like the Chinese delicacies, the sea-slugs, cut open and dried for keeping." For the most part, Holt's suggestions fell on deaf ears.

A, B6, K, niacin, riboflavin, and folate. It also contains the amino acids arginine and lysine at higher levels than in whole chicken eggs. Snail's low fat content (1.4 g per 100 g of snail meat) is respectable, compared with lean ground beef (18.3 g of fat per 100 g of flesh) and other, more conventional sources of animal protein.

As part of a study in Nigeria, young mothers and school-aged children were invited to taste-test pies made of *Achachatina marginata*, the largest of African snails, and pies made of beef. Most preferred the appearance, flavor, and texture of the ones baked with snails. "The snail pie is recommended as a cheap source of protein and iron for school-age children and young mothers, and could contribute in the fight against iron deficiency anemia," wrote the studies principal investigator, Ukpong Udofia of the University of Uyo.

SNAIL FARMING: DO AS THE ROMANS DO

Heliciculture, or snail farming, was first documented in 50 BC by the Greek historian Pliny the Elder, who wrote of the snail-rearing pens (called *cochlearia*) on the estate of one Fluvius Hirpinus, a citizen of Taquinium. According to Pliny, Hirpinus maintained a menagerie of land snail species: in one pen were the *albulae* from the town of Reate; in another, the very big snails from Illyria; a third pen contained African snails; and a fourth was occupied by snails from Soletum, noted for what Pliny claimed was their "nobility." Hirpinus fattened his stock with a diet of meal and new wine. What's not to like about that?

As their Empire spread, the Romans carried their mini-livestock with them, introducing them into the forests and fields of northern Europe—as evidenced by the numerous brown gardensnail and escargot snail shells found in kitchen waste excavated from Roman ruins throughout Great Britain. Long after the fall of the Roman Empire, both non-native *Helix* species were being plucked from gardens of convents and monasteries to be served as "meatless" meals during Lent.

Today's snail-farming nations include Indonesia, Greece, Morocco, China, Germany, Bulgaria, Yugoslavia, and Poland. France consumes more than 14,000 tons of snails every year, but practically none of these are domestically reared or harvested. With the most prized species protected by law, the French rely on central and east European imports to feed their cravings for escargot.

WORLDWIDE, SOME 11,600 TONNES of "Snails, Not Marine" were produced in 2008, according to the Food and Agriculture Organization of the United Nations.

29

ENDANGERED ESCARGOT

In England, the conversion of rural lands, coupled with overharvesting of wild escargot snails, brought naturalized populations of *Helix pomatia* to the edge of extinction. Nowadays, the escargot snail is one of ten mollusk species protected under Great Britain's Wildlife and Countryside Act. Enacted in 1981, this piece of legislation makes it illegal to kill, injure, collect, or sell this snail, making M. S. Lovell's book, *The Edible Mollusks of Great Britain and Ireland, With Recipes for Cooking Them*, a controversial tome 50 years after its publication.

Leave it to the French to escalate heliciculture to an art form. The first escargot recipe appeared in *Le Menagier du Paris*, a medieval manuscript circa 1394. It suggested that small snails with black shells be collected in the morning from the vines or elder trees, washed in salt and vinegar, removed from their shells, washed again, then stewed and served with bread.

Soldiers in Napoleon's army carried canned escargot as emergency rations during their great campaigns, and "the extract of 1,000 snails per man" was considered sufficient fare for a week's duty. French farmers maintained special *escagotieres*, or snail-preserves, in the corners of their vegetable gardens. The preserves were enclosed by thick hedges of parsley—a key ingredient in *escargot a la Bourgogne*.

Paris loves the dish. If you notice what workmen are eating in the modest restaurants of the busier quarters, you will for the next month or two find snails on five out of six plates. They are said to possess great nutritive value and to be almost a specific against consumption, so, notwithstanding their unattractive appearance, they are highly esteemed by rich and poor alike, and vast numbers are consumed every Winter.

—"WHEN SNAILS COME TO PARIS,"
The New York Times, November 14, 1909

Grow Your Own Escargot

Gastropod gastronomes maintain that, like oysters, snails should be eaten only in the "R" months—in particular, September, October, and November—before *Helix* species cease their feasting on garden greens and settle down for a long winter's nap. Gardeners who collect them in the spring will likely find little difference in flavor.

The snails can be easily gathered at this time of year. As the weather cools, they will congregate on sun-warmed surfaces

31

of outbuildings and rock walls, making them ripe for the plucking. Or they can also be lured to bait stations made of small piles of bran, placed beneath tipped-over flowerpots. After they've gorged on the bran, the snails will attach themselves to the insides of the pots, as if awaiting collection. Gather as many as you need for one meal (figure six to twelve snails per serving, depending on size).

It's only common sense but, nonetheless, should be restated here: avoid collecting edible snails in areas where pesticides or insecticides are or have been in use.

Captives can be kept in a five-gallon, food-grade plastic bucket with a tight-fitting lid, with numerous small holes drilled in it for ventilation. They can be fed lettuce (the French favor grape leaves) or fattened with cornmeal, bran, or high-protein soy meal for ten days. Withhold food—but not water *or* wine—for three days prior to serving.

Rinse the snails thoroughly in cool water. In a large bowl, ideally with a tight-fitting lid, cover them with water mixed with two tablespoons of salt and one tablespoon of vinegar per dozen snails. This will make the snails shed their slime, a process that can take up to 4 hours. By changing the solution frequently, the prep time can be reduced—but, hey, what's the rush?

Again, rinse the snails before tossing them into boiling lightly salted water. Simmer for 10 minutes, then drain the snails and allow them to cool. With a nutpick or crochet hook, remove the wee beasties from their shells. This may be difficult, because gardensnails often have thin, easily shattered shells. For this reason, it may be helpful to use grosblanc (*Helix pomatia*) shells, sold at gourmet shops or kitchen stores as coquilles.

Simmer the extracted meats slowly, over low heat, in a mixture of water and white wine, seasoned with salt, pepper, thyme, carrots, onions, and chopped garlic. After 2–3 hours (depending on size), remove them with a slotted spoon. Place each morsel in an empty, prewashed coquille. Fill any vacant spaces with a mixture of butter, seasoning, and parsley (historically, proportions and seasonings used have varied from district to district in France).

Place the filled shells into a baking pan. Wedge them in securely, or use crumpled aluminum foil, so the shells won't topple or roll around in the oven. Bake for 10 minutes at 450°F (about 200°C). When the butter has melted, serve at once—ideally with a loaf of French bread and a bottle of *Bourgogne Aligoté*, a dry white wine from Burgundy, the former snail-farming region of France.

CHAPTER II

A Gastropod Gallery

OREGON
FORESTSNAIL
*Allogona
townsendiana*

GROVESNAIL
Cepaea nemoralis

PACIFIC
SIDEBAND
*Monadenia
fidelis*

BROWN
GARDENSNAIL
Helix aspersa

NORTHWEST
HESPERION
*Vespericola
columbianus*

To err is human, to
slime sublime.

—*FIELD GUIDE TO THE SLUG* (1995)

Slowly but determinedly, the ancestors of today's snails and slugs slimed their way across the land, alternately dodging glaciers and lava flows, to find habitable niches in the Western states. As long-established links in the great chain of life, they perform several important roles, as gardeners, recyclers, and food sources for shrew moles, carabid beetles, and many other small animals.

Non-native species were transported to and, in at least one instance, intentionally dumped into the same environment within the past century or two. Participants in this second wave of settlement have easily adapted to the plant communities, weather conditions, and perturbations of humankind. Some of these recent arrivals are aggressive, driving away native snails and slugs to eventually dominate forested or farmed sites. Several kick the hostility up a notch, actively pursuing, dispatching, and ingesting the indigenous gastropod fauna.

Having left behind their historic nemeses—certain snail-eating thrushes or predacious tiger beetles—in the old country, the non-native snails and slugs are freer to breed and more likely to succeed than their native counterparts. Most of them evolved on the same Mediterranean, Eurasian, and northern European soils as our present-day vegetables and flowers. As such, they are predisposed to graze on our prized gladiolas and precious coriander starts. Alternatively, native snail and slug species evolved on the Pacific coast of what is now the United States and Canada and are less interested, food-wise, in the vegetables and flowers that we, relative newcomers to their world, tend to cultivate. Their bills of fare include native mosses, fungi, and leaf litter, and, in the case of the banana slug, a salad bar of native greenery—a total of nineteen different native plant species, by one biologist's count.

The parade of non-native slugs and snails crossing state and provincial borders is continuous, despite the best efforts of the Animal and Plant Health Inspection Service (APHIS)—Plant Protection and Quarantine, a branch of the U.S. Department of Agriculture. Within one five-year period, APHIS inspectors made over 4,900 molluscan interceptions on commodities, representing 396 gastropod species and sub-species belonging to 197 genera with origins from almost 100 countries.

Thus, to promote biodiversity and preserve healthy, fully integrated wild habitats, it's essential to recognize native pulmonates and, if possible, to respect their needs (even if they conflict with your plans to turn patches of weeds into manicured gardens). It's equally important to keep a close watch on non-native pulmonates' populations and, if necessary, take protective measures and, periodically, launch preemptive strikes to curb their growth.

Recognizing one type of land slug or snail from the rest is not nearly as difficult an endeavor as one might think. Nonetheless, it may take some study, at a library or online, along with a few snail-watching field trips, before one can readily distinguish the key species, both native and non-native, without eyestrain. This section offers brief profiles of some of the most accessible pulmonate species. More detailed information on a larger assortment of land-dwelling gastropods can be found in *Land Snails of British Columbia* by Robert G. Forsyth, a publication of the Royal BC Museum in Victoria, British Columbia.

The Art of Snail-Watching

There are several compelling reasons for watching land snails and slugs. Curiosity is as good a motive as any; the better your understanding of the food web (of which both you and the invertebrates are a part), the greater your appreciation of nature's grand design. Once again, recall the words of John Muir, who wrote that "in every walk with nature, one receives far more than he seeks." Truly, by watching the pulmonates in a garden, you're likely to learn only the habits of a few pesky introduced species—the ones that are more comfortable in disturbed habitats and slightly overwatered backyards. Although searching for native land snails in their natural habitats requires a greater expenditure of energy and time, it can offer greater rewards: rare glimpses of exceptional beings, each living in peaceful coexistence with the fungi, plants, and animals of their slow-paced worlds.

> *Never a day passes but that I do*
> *myself the honor to commune with*
> *some of nature's varied forms.*
>
> —GEORGE WASHINGTON CARVER

Because most native slugs and snails are solitary by nature, there is a greater likelihood of encountering single specimens than whole herds. Nonetheless, once you've discovered a woodland species' favorite spot, you can revisit it over several seasons, as most of these creatures are territorial—that is, they tend to stay within easy crawling distance of a cozy den. In his book *The Shell Makers: Introducing Mollusks*, Alan Solem estimates that the movements of a land snail are confined to a 20-foot (6-m) radius.

Many slugs show strong attachments to particular shelters during hot or dry weather, but tend to relocate during cool, moist weather. Comfortably wedged in a rock crevice or beneath a stone or a log, the banana slug can wait out a dry spell, remaining in a torpid state for more than three months. At higher altitudes, slugs of the genus *Prophysaon* may remain cooped up in a hollow log for as long as six or seven months. If you find either of these stay-at-homes in their dormant states, let them be. Forcing them out of their torpor could cost them their lives.

Reclusive snail species may also congregate on sun-warmed stone walls, in the moss-covered crotches of deciduous trees, under paving stones, and beneath felled logs. During winter months, they may huddle together, their close proximity helping to conserve metabolic heat, in what scientists call a *hibernaculum*—a word that, like *Sanctum Sanctorum*, conjures up images of Dr. Caligari or the late Vincent Price.

NIGHTTIME IS THE RIGHT TIME

With a few exceptions, snails and slugs are most active at night. To observe them in action during these moments, go into your garden after dark or shortly before sunup, armed with a flashlight or, better yet, a headlamp, which will leave both hands free to gather any uninvited guests. Garden slugs and snails are most rapacious during months with moderate but consistent rainfall and nighttime temperatures above 50 degrees Fahrenheit (10°C). Generally, throughout the Pacific Northwest and northern California, the best months to mount a non-native snail safari are March, April, May, June, October, and early November. However, even in the coldest or driest weather, it should be possible to find some evidence of nighttime activity.

By becoming more familiar with the land mollusks' patterns for raiding your garden, you will be more capable of limiting damage to your plants. By periodically conducting informal surveys of abundance, you should get an idea of the most practical and effective control strategies. Increased numbers, especially of young slugs or snails, will serve as a warning that sterner controls are needed.

Before you return the snail to its natural environment, examine the skin with your pocket magnifier. It will remind you of an alligator's skin—rough and divided into plates with a surface like pebbled leather.

—RICHARD HEADSTROM,
Adventures with a Hand Lens (c. 1962)

The Shell Game

The formal boundary between "slugdom" and "snaildom" is somewhat arbitrary. However, few people would have difficulty pegging the snail in a lineup of slugs.

The obvious difference, of course, is the shell. Without it, one West Coast snail species looks pretty much like the next. Therefore, identification is usually based on the attributes of a snail's shell, rather than its skin color or body proportions. Identifying individual shells from their unique characteristics requires that one learn the specialized language of conchology. A few basic terms are presented in the illustration on the next page.

All West Coast land snail shells are turbinate—that is, they grow at an angle along a spiral axis. Each revolution around this axis is known as a whorl, and the tip of the spire is called its apex. The juncture of each whorl against the other forms a suture. The circular hollow often created by the spiraling whorls is the umbilicus. The aperture is the opening into which a live snail can retreat. The edge of the body whorl that borders the aperture is known as the lip or, more technically, the peristome. The columnar edge is the inner edge of this lip, and the outer edge is the margin.

The openings of many adult snail shells display minute toot-like features called *apertural denticles*. The exact purpose of these features has been hotly debated, with an

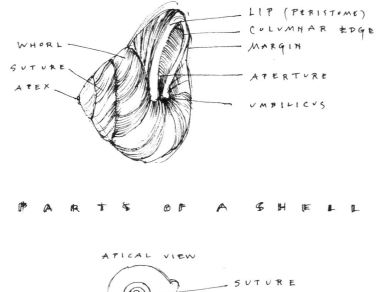

LIP (PERISTOME)
COLUMNAR EDGE
MARGIN
WHORL
APERTURE
SUTURE
APEX
UMBILICUS

P A R T S   O F   A   S H E L L

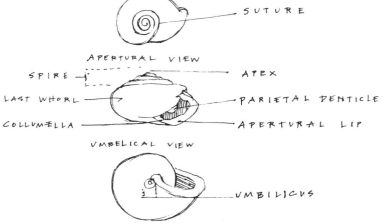

APICAL VIEW
SUTURE

APERTURAL VIEW
SPIRE
APEX
LAST WHORL
PARIETAL DENTICLE
COLLUMELLA
APERTURAL LIP

UMBELICAL VIEW
UMBILICUS

As in other branches of science, the language of conchology is quite specific; each feature of the land snail's shell has its own name, facilitating easeful description.

assortment of suggestions, from protection from predators to support for the snail's soft body parts. Regardless of their utility, the numbers and arrangements of apertural teeth can be aids in species identification.

The majority of turbinate shells are dextral. While holding a shell with its opening facing you and its tip facing up, the opening is on the right side. If you should happen to find a shell with a left-sided opening, hang on to it. It could be valuable, if not to science then at least to an amateur collector.

Time and Patience would
bring the snail to Jerusalem.

—IRISH PROVERB

COLLECTING SNAIL SHELLS

It's easy to gather, prepare and display an assortment of snail shells, an enterprise that, like stamp collecting, can fast become a fixation. Most land snail shells are small, requiring less display space than collection of Indian blankets, Roseville pottery, duck decoys, or, for that matter, most seashells. On the other hand, the size and fragility of land snail shells makes their display a challenge. They can be securely kept in printer's type trays (sold in antique stores and curio shops), or more formally presented in what are known to butterfly collectors as Riker mounts—shallow, glass-covered boxes made of cardboard and filled with a layer of cotton. These are available from BioQuip, Carolina Biological, and other scientific suppliers.

You can purchase land snail shells at specialty stores or online on eBay and other commercial sites. Swap meets hosted by local shell clubs are also good places to acquire these calcareous gems. Perhaps the simplest and most satisfactory way to enlarge a collection is by gathering land snails, either dead or alive, and cleaning the shells by yourself.

Detailed instructions for cleaning shells are contained in *Compendium of Land Snails* by R. Tucker Abbott and summarized here. Live snails should be deposited in Ziploc bags, placed in a freezer for 24 hours, and allowed to thaw. This may be the most humane way to dispatch cold-blooded animals, as a sudden freeze forces these animals to drift off into a deep sleep from which they never awaken. The dead snails can be defrosted, transferred to a pan of water and boiled for a minute or two. This solidifies the snails' slippery meat, which can then be teased from the shell with a safety pin or dissecting needle. There's only one drawback to this method: hot water can fade some of the colors in snail shells. For this reason, some collectors place their defrosted snails in ceramic or glass containers and microwave them for about 3 minutes on a high setting.

This causes the soft-bodied occupant to pop out while leaving the shell's subtle hues intact.

To preserve slug specimens for show-and-tell, malacologist Frank Collins Baker has suggested drowning the captives—a maneuver that, he maintained, will result in "the eye peduncles and tentacles being stretched out to their fullest extent." The carcasses are next subjected to progressively stronger solutions of ethanol: 30 percent for 24 hours, 70 percent for 30 hours, and 85 percent for final preservation. Fully pickled, the slugs in glass jars make outstanding conversation-starters, enabling you to share your newly acquired knowledge of the pulmonate mollusks.

Some Common Non-Native Snails

We'll begin our tour of the gastropod menagerie with some of the more conspicuous specimens and, ironically, some of the most thoroughly studied of the pulmonate mollusks. These are the non-native "guests" in our gardens. To know them is not necessarily to love them.

GROVESNAIL

The grovesnail (*Cepaea nemoralis*) came to North America from Western Europe, first establishing itself in gardens in several eastern provinces and states. "In 1857, I imported some hundred living specimens from near Sheffield, England, and freed them in my garden in Burlington, New Jersey," wrote one avid gardener in 1865. "They have thriven well and increased with great rapidity, so that now the whole town is full of them."

There have been many accidental introductions of this beautifully colored land snail since then. Because of its ease of acquisition, the grovesnail is often used for laboratory trials. It's quite possible that releases of surplus snails at the conclusion of such experiments may have aided this species' dispersal. This species is now well established in many urban and suburban gardens.

The grovesnail's one-inch-diameter (2.5 cm) shells come in shades of red, yellow, and olive, with one to five bands of cinnamon to chocolate brown hues. The shell's brown lip usually distinguishes its wearer from the white-lipped grovesnail (*Cepaea hortensis*) an equally common introduced species.

In 2009, the year of Charles Darwin's bicentenary, people throughout Europe and North Africa were asked to collect grovesnails and share information about the colors and numbers of bands on the shells of the snails.

Participants in this survey could go to a Web site to post this info. By comparing the shell patterns to those of snails from other parts of the continent, participants could identify trends in *Cepaea* shell variation—and see Darwinian evolution in action.

"It may look like banded snails are dressed-to-kill, but really they are dressed not to be killed," the Web site explained. Because grovesnails are a favored food of the song thrush (*Turdus philomelos*), shell markings serve as effective camouflage, helping the gastropods to conceal themselves against different backgrounds, thus avoiding detection by this keen-sighted predator. Where song thrushes are no longer abundant, the need to blend in is not as important anymore. In addition, by absorbing sunlight and storing heat, the dark-colored shells may be helpful for grovesnails in northern climes. Scientists theorize that lighter-colored shells may now be more common in these latitudes, primarily due to climate change.

BROWN GARDENSNAIL

Credit for at least one introduction of the brown gardensnail (*Helix aspersa*) goes to Antoine Delmas, founder of a San Jose, California, vineyard. It's said that Delmas so sorely pined for *escargots forestières* (forest snails in garlic butter) from his native France that, in 1859, he acquired a batch of exotic snails, possibly from the same supplier of his Black St. Peter (Zinfandel) vines. To ensure a consistent supply, Delmas also planted his imported snails within the city limits of San Francisco and Los Angeles.

"The San Francisco planting was probably a failure," wrote malacologist Robert E. C. Stearns, author of *Exotic Mollusca in California*, nearly fifty years after Delmas's feat. In Stearns's opinion, the "cold sea winds, fog, sanddunes, and shifting sands and sparse, ligneous, scrubby vegetation" of the still largely unsettled Queen City would have been challenging to the gourmet gastropod's naturalization. Somehow, the snails found cozy niches in the New World. In April, 1900, when *Science* published Stearns's piece, the brown gardensnail had taken permanent residences in the flower beds of nearby Oakland, as well as the backyards of Pacific Grove, more than 50 miles south of the Delmas estate. Today, these natives of Western Europe and the Mediterranean region have extended their range to a variety of urban, suburban, and rural settings in the U.S as well as in Cuba, Haiti, South America, South Africa, Australia, and New Zealand.

In France, from where the *Helix aspersa* hails, this snail is known as the *petit gris* ("small gray") to distinguish it from a much larger and, purportedly, tastier relative, *Helix pomatia*, the *gros blanc* ("large white") or Burgundy snail. The light brown shell of this species is conical with a blunt spire, irregularly marked with growth lines and sculpted

A CLOSE RELATIVE of the brown gardensnail, the Roman Snail, *Helix pomatia*, is popularly known as the apple snail. Its Latin species name, although appropriate considering the shape of its shell, was not derived from the Latin word *pomum*, an apple, but from the Greek *poma*, signifying a lid or covering—in other words, an operculum.

with folds, barely more than 1⅛ inches (2.9 cm) in diameter. Its white-lipped margin has an outwardly bent edge; the umbilicus is completely covered by the columnar edge.

"Strange to say, epicures who like snails for food seem to prefer them from imported cans from Europe rather than picking them from western gardens," offers G. Dallas Hanna, whose 1966 monograph *Introduced Mollusks of Western North America* remains invaluable for snail sorters to this day.

GARLIC GLASS-SNAIL

The garlic glass-snail (*Oxychilus alliarius*) is a quarter-inch (6 mm) member of a large European family of thin-shelled mollusks, the Daubebariidae, or glass-snails, as they are commonly called. As one might guess, the name comes from the shell's transparency—a feature less obvious in a living specimen, whose dark-gray to black body is highly visible inside the see-through shell.

Like a skunk, this pulmonate has the potential for producing a disagreeable odor when provoked. That odor, it turns out, is from a thick brown mucus secreted by large cells clustered near the pneumostome, on the right side of the mantle. The odor itself comes from proteinaceous material rich in sulfur compounds, mainly the highly aromatic thiol, 1-propanethiol. Most thiols have a garlicky smell. They are often used as warning odorant, whether as an additive to liquid propane gas and as the active ingredient in a skunk's defensive spray. Laboratory tests show that hedgehogs show a marked reversion to this little stinker. It's common knowledge that sulfur comes from food ingested by the snail. Which foods specifically remains a mystery.

In North America, the garlic glass-snail is largely dependent on humankind, enjoying the comfort of our greenhouses, cold frames, and cloches. Its glossy amber or horn-colored shell is streaked with dull gray and includes four to six rather flat whorls. Look for a small but obvious umbilicus. The cellar glass-snail (*O. cellarius*) is nearly identical in appearance, but is a bit bigger and does not produce an odor. How it wards off hedgehogs has yet to be determined. Both species are opportunistic feeders; they eat earthworms, live and dead (decaying) plant material, and other pulmonates gastropods as well as their eggs.

DECOLLATE SNAIL

The tapered, elongated inch-long (2.5 cm) shell of the decollate snail (*Rumina decollata*) facilitates identification of this Mediterranean animal in the field. This non-native feeds on other pulmonates and, for this reason, has been introduced into gardens in hopes of controlling the brown gardensnail and other pest snail and slug species. It is most effective at taking down small prey with (one-half-inch or 1.3 cm) diameter shells. Because decollate snails also eat young seedlings, they may not fully prove their worth within garden plots. However, in citrus groves, these molluscivores have significantly reduced brown gardensnail infestations within four to ten years. As an indiscriminate eater, the decollate snail can put non-pest snail populations at risk. For this reason, it can be legally introduced only in certain central and southern California county agricultural districts. Importation of this species is prohibited in Oregon, Washington, and British Columbia; the cold-blooded snail killers make rare appearances nonetheless.

A Fistful of Native Snails

Now, having encountered the enemy, it's time to familiarize ourselves with the less bothersome and, in many instances, more charismatic native snail species. Because they pose considerably less of a threat to our agricultural endeavors, most have not been subjects of exhaustive field and laboratory studies. Your observations as so-called "citizen scientists" could add significantly to our understanding of these oft-elusive animals.

PACIFIC SIDEBAND

The Pacific sideband (*Monadenia fidelis*) can be recognized by its handsome 1¼-inch (3.2 cm) nut-brown shell, streaked with light bands, dark bands, or both. It is the largest of land snails in the Pacific Northwest, with several related species occurring in Oregon and northern California. In winter, it seeks protection from cold under blankets of moss in the crotches of trees, and also hibernates under leaf litter at the bases of bigleaf maple (*Acer macrophyllum*) trees. The association with trees may be a key facet of this snail's life history: individuals have been observed creeping slowly in trees more than 21 feet (6.7 m) off the ground.

LANCETOOTH SPECIES

While the Haplotremidae are mainly a North American family, several members inhabit the West Indies, Central America, and northern South America. A total of fifteen species and subspecies inhabit West Coast habitats, from British Columbia to northern Baja California in Mexico. Members of this family are carnivores, dining almost exclusively on earthworms, other gastropods, and, yes, smaller-sized members of their own species. By extending its long narrow body, one of these snails can insinuate itself far into the shell of another snail, regardless of how far its pulmonate prey may withdraw. The common name for these animals, the lancetooths, refers to the harpoon-like, modified teeth of the radula—all the better to spear and dispatch other soft-bodied invertebrates.

The beaded lancetooth (*Ancotrema sportella*) has a light greenish-yellow shell roughly a half-inch (1.3 cm) in diameter, with a flattened spire and a pronounced concavity on one edge of its aperture lip. That flattened shell may be useful for its wearer to insinuate itself under logs, paving stones, and garden debris, and although this creature is fairly common, it is easily overlooked by scientists and nonscientists alike.

Ancotrema sportella shares its range (from northern California to Alaska) with a second carnivorous species, the robust lancetooth (*Haplotrema vancouverense*) whose

1¼-inch (3.2 cm) shell, while also prominently flattened and umbilicate, shows little indentation of the aperture lip.

A third Northwest species, the Oregon lancetooth (*Ancotrema hybridium*) was recently awarded species status by snail taxonomists. It is intermediate in size between *A. sportella* and *A. vancouverense*.

> *I own my humble life, good friend;*
> *Snail was I born, and snail shall end.*
>
> —JOHN GAY,
> "The Butterfly and the Snail,"
> in *Fifty-One Fables in Verse* (1727)

HESPERIAN SPECIES

More than twenty species of hesperian (*Verspicola*) snails have been identified from Central California to southern Alaska, with many species as-yet unnamed. In the living snail, the brown, ¾-inch-diameter (2 cm) shell of the Northwest hesperian (*Vespericola columbianus*) is covered with fine hairs. The hairs are catch-alls for dirt, assisting the snail with any efforts to blend in with the surrounding soils. The hairs fall off after the animal dies; in these hairless specimens, look for the aperture's thickened lip and, in some specimens, the presence of a single apertural tooth. The closely related *Vespericola pilosus* exists only in the San Francisco region of central California.

OREGON FORESTSNAIL

The Oregon forestsnail (*Allogona townsendiana*) and Idaho forestsnail (*A. ptychophora*) are relatives of *Vespericola*, and their large-diameter shells of 1.2 and 0.9 inches (3 cm and 2.4 cm), respectively, shares the same thickening of the lip. The gnarly whorls of its polished pecan-brown shell are often eroded, revealing a whitish, limy undercoat. Although well established in the U.S., the Oregon forest-snail has been listed as endangered on Canada's Wildlife Species at Risk, perhaps due to its dwindling habitat—a result of urban encroachment and the conversion of forests into agricultural lands. This beleaguered species seeks refuge in patches of stinging nettle (*Urtica dioica*) and among the thorny canes of salmonberry (*Rubus spectablis*) and thimbleberry (*R. parviflorus*).

Common Non-Native Slugs

Because of their peridomestic lifestyles, the introduced slugs species are most often sighted by West Coast gardeners at work. These gastropods are prolific, to say the least, and like rats or roaches, there is no such thing as "just one." If you've located a single specimen, keep looking until you've found and eliminated its brood mates.

> *Slugs are awful, slugs are things from*
> *the edges of insanity, and I am afraid of*
> *slugs and all their attributes.*

—M. F. K. FISHER,
"Fifty Million Snails,"
from *Serve It Forth* (1937)

CHOCOLATE ARION

The chocolate arion (*Arion rufus*) comes in many colors besides cocoa. The numerous ridges and furrows behind the mantle of this slug are better identifiers than its color. Reddish brown members of the species sport a striped red-orange skirt. A bit more than half the size of the biggest banana slug (5¾ inches or 15 cm) when in motion, the chocolate arion will work itself into an even smaller hillock when at rest. It will also curl into a ball

GREY FIELD SLUG
Deroceras reticulatum

CHOCOLATE ARION
Arion rufus

WARTY JUMPING-SLUG
Hemphillia glandulosa

GIANT GARDEN SLUG
Limax maximus

BANANA SLUG
Ariolimax columbianus

and rock back and forth when under attack. It has been estimated that, at times, *Arion rufus* has damaged more than 75 percent of Washington's strawberry crop. In some parts of Washington's Mount Baker National Forest, chocolate arions outnumber the banana slugs two-to-one. Personally, I sighted five specimens of *Arion rufus*, but only two of the banana slug along a half-mile path to a beach on Orcas Island, Washington.

Eight smaller *Arion* species (under 1½ inches or 4 cm) also exist in the Northwest: *A. circumscriptus*, *A. distinctus*, *A. fasciaus*, *A. hortensis*, *A. intermedius*, *A. owenii*, *A. silvaticus*, and *A. subfuscus*. Six of these are also found in California's slug-friendly climes. None is native to North America. *A. distinctus* is quite cosmopolitan, practically a domestic animal, rarely seen outside gardens and metropolitan parks.

Why was this slug genera named after Arion of Corinth, an ancient Greek poet? To quote Dr. Seuss, "I do not know. Go ask your dad."

> *If you have to hate anything, let it be this slug,*
> *a cruelly destructive pest if ever there was one.*
>
> —EUGENE N. KOZLOFF,
> *Plants and Animals of the*
> *Pacific Northwest* (1976)

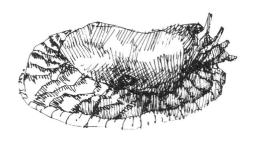

ARION rufus

The plasticity of slugs such as Arion rufus (shown here in three commonly encountered modes) can make it hard for novice gastropod watchers to distinguish one species from the next.

GIANT GARDENSLUG

The giant gardenslug (*Limax maximus*) is one of the keeled slugs, with a signature ridge running about a third of its body length. Frequently encountered in West Coast gardens, it comes by its common name honestly. Sporting a leopard's spots or a tiger's stripes on its mantle and the upper surface of its foot, the giant gardenslug can be distinguished up close by its keel, its smooth, unfurrowed body, and the placement of the pneumostome, which, unlike the chocolate arion's, is located near the rear edge of the mantle. A relative of the giant gardenslug, the ash-black gardenslug (*Limax cineroniger*) is the largest slug species known to science, reaching a length of slightly under one foot (30 cm).

Although considerably smaller than the banana slug, this 4–8-inch (10–20 cm) invader from Asia Minor and Europe can crawl four times faster. In the Northwest, it is one of a handful of cannibalistic slugs (perhaps giving the comparatively mild-mannered native slugs a good reason to race). If you find a dying slug on a city sidewalk at sunup, it might not be just a stray caught by the morning sun, but perhaps a victim of a giant gardenslug attack.

Limax maximus was so named by Carl Linnaeus, father of modern systematics, in 1758. One hundred and thirty-two years later, a specimen was identified by Charles Russell Orcutt, having been collected in San Diego. Three years later, in 1893, this species had also left its heart in San Francisco, according to malacologist William M. Wood.

One may often notice numbers of a minute white parasitic mite . . . running about the body of this slug, and it is said also to live in the respiratory cavity, but does not appear to cause annoyance or injury to its host.

—RICHARD LYDEKKER,
The New Natural History, Volume VI (1901)

GREY FIELDSLUG

An import from northern Europe and Asia, the grey fieldslug (*Deroceras reticulatum*) is about 2 inches (5 cm) long, generally light brown or gray, with darker mottling and a boat-like keel that ends abruptly at the tail. Some specimens are almost white. A distinct feature of this species is its milky slime, which it produces in copious quantities when irritated. An equally strong identifier is the series of small, concentric folds in the mantle.

Like the chocolate arion, the grey fieldslug has become a serious pest in parts of Washington, Oregon, and California. It can slither its way into the center of a cabbage and then gorge itself on the walls of the vegetable. Grey fieldslugs have been indicted for damage to grain fields, strawberries, and vegetable crops in the Puyallup Valley of Washington and the Willamette Valley of Oregon.

The meadow fieldslug (*Deroceras laeve*) and evening fieldslug (*Deroceras hesperium*) are the only members of this genus that are native to the Pacific Northwest. The one-ridge fieldslug (*Deroceras monentolophus*) has been reported in Seattle, which seems odd, considering that the rest of its distribution is from Mendocino County to southern California.

EARSHELL SLUG

The non-native earshell slug (*Testacella haliotidea*) is a carnivore, with a harpoon-like barbed radula for impaling earthworms and other soft-bodied prey. The catch is swallowed whole, an act that takes several hours to complete. Much of this slug's life is spent underground. Its small size—less than 2½ inches (6 cm)—and subdued gray-brown or pale yellow skin make it easy to overlook. One characteristic stands out, however: a small, cap-like shell resembling that of an abalone. It is from this feature that this species of *Testacella* gets its name, *haliotidea*—a reference to the abalone genus, *Haliotis*.

It has been likened to the tiger and the shark, in its cunning while pursuing its prey, and in its ferocity when attacking it. The poor earthworm stands but a slight chance of escape when Testacella scents it and starts its pursuit. The earthworm tries to escape by retreating into its underground galleries; but this is of no avail, because the mollusk has a long, narrow body, and can go wherever the worm does. If the worm, perchance, has the opportunity of retreating far into its galleries, the mollusk will dig tunnels to intercept it. Frequently the mollusk will make a sudden spring upon its victim, taking it by surprise.

—FRANK COLLINS BAKER,
Shells of Land and Water (c. 1903)

GREENHOUSE SLUG

The drab, gray greenhouse slug (*Milax gagates*) is actually a true world traveler, with specimens discovered in locales as remote as Easter Island. Unintentionally carried to the Northwest from Mediterranean climes, the greenhouse slug thrives in a warm, stable environment, making it the scourge of indoor gardeners throughout the Northwest. Even if you leave the door to your greenhouse wide open, this slug will seldom venture outside. Rather, it will burrow into the first few inches of greenhouse soil and feast almost exclusively on the roots of your favorite plants. A key identifier for this species is a sharp dorsal keel that runs from the mantle to the tip of the tail. Look for a small horseshoe- or diamond-shaped groove in the center of the mantle. Like all members of their genus, greenhouse slugs sport the rudiments of a small spiral shell, completely enclosed by the skin of the mantle. Freshly hatched milacids are fully enclosed in this shell, but they soon outgrow it in their rush to become 2¾-inch (7 cm) adults. The greenhouse slug was called "one of the most destructive garden pests of California" by G. Dallas Hanna in the 1966 report, "Introduced Mollusks of Western North America."

An Abundance of Native Slugs

Native slugs are contributors as well as consumers, playing many key roles in their natural settings. They are the underdogs of the invertebrate world, worth rooting for, even while they are trespassing in our garden plots. After all, to err is human, to slime, sublime.

BANANA SLUGS

Native to the Pacific Northwest and northern California, the banana slug (genus *Ariolimax*) can grow to a length of 8 inches (20 cm), with a few giants reaching 10 inches (25.4 cm) and weights of a quarter pound (0.1 kg).

This mega-mollusk is the second-largest slug in the world. Its color ranges from plain white to black, with many intermediate color forms—lemon yellow, light tan, and dark brown—often with black blotches or spots. In the early 1900s, each color variation was described as a new species. Today, though, only three species of banana slugs are recognized by scientists: *Ariolimax columbianus*, *A. dolichophallus*, and *A. californicus*. The most widely distributed of the three is *A. columbianus*, which lives almost exclusively in forested habitats of southeast Alaska, British Columbia, Washington, Oregon, and northern California. These three species are less frequently encountered in urban areas.

Any slug watcher unable to identify the banana slug by its coloring, great size, or preference for woodland locales

IN 1999, THE U.S. POSTAL SERVICE issued a sheet of 33-cent stamps depicting rainforest plants and animals—including a sporty green banana slug on a bed of moss.

should look for a third distinguishing trait: a small indentation (called the *caudal pore*) at the tip of the slug's tail,
typically capped with a mucous plug. The mucus from
this pore seems to deter rear-end attacks from shrews,
shrew moles, and predaceous beetles. It's apparently not
too much of a deterrent for *Ariolimax*, however, which, if
particularly hungry, will eat its own plug or, prior to pairing off, nibble at the plug of a prospective mate.

Adult banana slugs have a rather long reproductive
period, from late summer through early spring, which
coincides with the Northwest's wet months. An individual banana slug can lay up to forty pearly white eggs, each
protected by a hard outer shell. Eggs laid in late autumn
usually overwinter and hatch the next spring. From these
5/16-inch-diameter orbs come miniature versions of their
parents. These youngsters grow rapidly and add weight
throughout their six-year lifespan as gastropod goliaths.

In the mid-1980s, students at the University of
California, Santa Cruz, chose the banana slug over the
sea lion for their campus' official mascot, reportedly by a
15-to-1 margin. Since then, the bespectacled Sammy the
Slug has made in-person appearances at sports events, and
has figured prominently in numerous T-shirt designs. In
print, Sammy is often reading a volume of Plato, and is
linked to the university's motto, "Fiat Slug." In 1994, when
John Travolta donned one of these shirts in the film *Pulp
Fiction*, demand far exceeded supply, and the campus

bookstore was forced to turn away would-be buyers for several months while a new batch of T-shirts was printed. When the Grateful Dead gifted their archive of recorded material to the UC Santa Cruz library in 2008, a special Grateful Slug T-shirt was produced and sold to help defray the cost of maintaining the collection.

TAILDROPPER SLUGS

The name *Prophysaon* means "forward-breathing," and refers to the placement of the pneumostome, in the front portion of the mantle of slugs in this genus. Slugs that are classified as *Prophysaon* are commonly called taildroppers, having gained a reputation for what scientists call autotomy—that is, when attacked by a predator, they can jettison part of their tail. A yellow-green mucus is secreted on the front section of the body at the site of the attack. Assumed to be a deterrent, this sticky substance may divert further attacks from the body and toward the detached tail. Ideally, the 2¼-inch-long (6 cm) slug will then make its escape. Under laboratory conditions, a new tail is regenerated in approximately five weeks. The autotomized section is packed with glycogen cells, which are stored nutrients that can be used by the slug if food is unavailable.

Dark gray with lateral bands of color, the scarletback taildropper (*Prophysaon vanattae*) is a tree-hugger, favoring the moss-covered bark and branches of trees and shrubs in mixed forests throughout British Columbia, Washington, and northwestern Oregon. It is 1–1½ inches (25–40 mm) long.

In excess of 4 inches (100 mm) in length, the yellow-bordered taildropper (*P. foliolatum*) is the largest member of this genus, typically yellowish, with a light stripe down its back and several dark brown streaks and spots. However, specimens collected from a single leaf of western skunk cabbage (*Lysichiton americanus*) on the Olympic coast of Washington showed a range of body colors—from very pale yellow without markings to dark rust or brown. Therefore, it is better to use the tail as an identifier of this and other related species. Shaped more or less like a rounded oblong, it usually bears a small crease marking the site where self-amputation takes place. In species where this crease is not visible, look for a fine white line across the sole of the foot.

Overall, it may be concluded that the autotomy response is a highly organized and stable mechanism of defense. Its persistence in the genus Prophysaon, despite its presumed high cost [i.e., the loss of one's tail], suggests that the response contributes significantly to the survival of slugs in nature.

—INGRITH DEYRUP-OLSEN,
A. W. MARTIN, AND R. T. PAINE,
"The Autonomy Escape Response of the Terrestrial
Slug *Prophysaon foliatum*," in *Malacologica* (1986)

The reticulate taildropper (*P. andersoni*) has diamond-shaped patterns on its back, not unlike the reticulated python. It seldom exceeds 2⅓ inches (60 mm). The blue-grey taildropper (*P. coeruleum*) is only 1¾ inches (45 mm) and, because of its color, is easily distinguished from other small slugs. Look for it in stands of bigleaf maple (*Acer macrophyllum*) or other deciduous trees.

The blue-grey taildropper is apparently a rare species in Washington and northwestern Oregon. Further south in Oregon, it is more common and may occupy a broader range of environments. However, within the southern part of its range, other variants or species occur that may be responsible for the broader ecological amplitude in that area.

JUMPING-SLUG SPECIES

Considerably smaller than most Northwest native slugs (½ to ¾ inch, or 13 to 20 mm), members of the jumping-slug genus *Hemphillia* can be distinguished by their vestigial shells, the edges of which are partly blurred by the skin of the mantle. These mottled olive-and-brown natives avoid predators by resorting to invertebrate acrobatics. A resting slug will wrap its long, slender tail forward around its body. If disturbed, it will swing the tail back, twisting and writhing with such vigor that the slug often jumps an inch. The adaptive range of one species, *Hemphillia dromedarius*, the dromedary jumping-slug, is impressive: in Oregon, specimens have been collected deep in the Columbia Gorge and on Mount Hood at elevations up to 4,250 feet (1,295 m). A relative, the warty jumping-slug (*H. glandulosa*), is found solely in coastal forests, a few feet above sea level. The pale jumping-slug (*H. camelus*) is the most widespread member of this genus in British Columbia.

> *Niagara Falls!*
> *Slowly he turns.*
> *The little snail.*
>
> —BARRY ROTH

Keeping Pulmonates as Pets

For patient observers of nature, slugs and snails can make excellent companions. Admittedly, they won't retrieve the Sunday paper, nor will they climb onto their owner's lap and demand to be scratched behind the ears. Nonetheless, like tropical fish, they can provide hours of passive entertainment and require minimal care. It's not uncommon for captive slugs and snails to mate and lay eggs in their artificial environments. In such instances, the rewards of waiting and watching closely will include a dozen or more hatchlings, which can be shared with others or reintroduced to their wild habitat, just like Elsa the lion in *Born Free*.

Begin with a fish tank, 10 gallons (38 l) or larger. Cover the base of the tank with an inch (2.5 cm) of pea gravel for drainage, and then add an inch or two of sterilized potting soil. Now decorate with moss, leaf litter, and twigs. Add a couple of pieces of tree bark, a few rocks, or some pot shards to make hiding places; these hide-outs will encourage your pulmonate pets to stay put instead of roaming and sliming the aquarium's glass. Over time, slime trails will eventually obscure the view, so it's best to remove them, preferably after they've dried, with a razor blade, followed by a moist cloth or paper towel (as explained on page 119, using a wet sponge or squeegee will only make matters worse).

Make sure you buy or build a snug-fitting screen top for the tank, as without it the occupants should have no difficulty climbing straight up and out. The screen top will allow air to circulate, keeping the tank's moist interior fresh. Because pulmonates favor damp conditions, at least half of the screening should be covered with cardboard or foil, which will keep some moisture in. From time to time, as needed, you may want to use a plant mister to increase humidity.

If for no other reasons than its spectacular size and docile temperament, a banana slug is a good pet for a child. They are extremely heat-sensitive, though, making them less suited to captive lifestyles than the many introduced snail and slug species, which have proved their adaptability time and again. For cold-loving species, keep their tank on an unheated porch or in a garage. They should be brought indoors during severe cold spells and returned only when the temperatures are well above freezing.

More tolerant of heat, the giant gardenslug and the grovesnail make better pets. A drawback to the giant gardenslug is, alas, its nocturnal nature: the most entertaining moments are likely to occur at night, when no one is around to notice.

Pet snails and slugs should be offered a broad spectrum of foods—spinach, lettuce, and other leafy greens—augmented with fresh browse, harvested from the outdoors. Personal experience has shown that many pulmonates have a fondness for yams, but tend to reject scraps of sweet potato or regular potato. Other gastropod staples include dry kibbled dog food or cat food, poultry mash, and pelleted goldfish food. Rolled oats may appeal to detritivorous snails and slugs; a teaspoon of powdered milk added to the rolled oats makes a nice calcium supplement. Don't assume that all slug and snail fare must be fresh; in most cases, overripe and wilted fruits and vegetables (which often can be obtained free of charge from produce stands) will be eaten with gusto.

Snails and slugs have few medical disorders, so it is altogether possible for individuals kept in captivity to live as long as several years, depending on the species. Like everyone else, the pulmonates are susceptible to bacterial infections, but, with the exception of salmonella, these are not transmittable to humans or other endothermic (warm-blooded) occupants of your home. Because salmonella infections can pose serious health threats, thorough hand washing is highly recommended after handling these pets, their food dishes, and any materials with which the slugs and snails make contact. Some snail and slug species are intermediate hosts to flukes and other parasites, and for this reason alone, it is never a good idea to kiss your pet—as if you had even a fleeting thought of doing so!

CHAPTER III

Seven Wonders of Snaildom

Some people may be repelled by the thought of slugs fornicating, but there is an unusual carnal beauty involved which is worth looking into.

—MASAMUNE SHIROW,
creator of *Ghost in the Shell* (1989), a popular manga

Albeit less photogenic than the Pyramid of Giza and considerably smaller than the Colossus of Rhodes, land slugs and snails deserve to be placed among the wonders of the world. Their many unusual attributes and odd behaviors are briefly presented in the following essays. It is the author's intent to reveal the secrets of the pulmonates' success in biological terms . . . and to give the reader additional topics to think about late at night.

Speed (or Lack Thereof)

To distinguish them from virtually instantaneous e-mail messages, we call actual letters delivered by the postal service "snail mail." But is that term entirely accurate? Not according to a Reuters news story from January 2008.

The Reuters report shared the story of Michal Szybalsky, an IT worker in Poland who received a letter on January 3, 2008, that was sent thirteen days earlier, on December 20, 2007, by priority mail. He calculated that a snail would have covered the distance from the letter's sender and its receiver, a span of 6.89 miles (11.1 km), with much greater speed.

Polish mail carriers took 294 hours to deliver the letter, which traveled at an average speed of what pencils out to be 0.0236 miles (0.038 km) per hour. An average-sized snail, traveling at an estimated 0.3 miles per hour could have covered the same distance in 227 hours, or a little under nine-and-a-half days.

One might question whether a snail in the employ of the Polish postal service could withstand the sheer weight of a priority letter. It should be pointed out that, while undeniably slow, snails and slugs are remarkably strong. In laboratory tests, one snail species was able to drag fifty times its own weight horizontally and nine times its weight vertically. Now *you* try that.

I want to thank you for putting
me back in my snail shell.

I want to thank you for putting
me back in my snail shell.

—"SNAIL SHELL,"
They Might Be Giants

WILL SPRINT FOR FOOD

With food as a motivator, even the smallest of slugs and snails can cover great distances. The grey fieldslug, for example, will travel up to 40 feet (12.2 m) in a single night to get its fill. Finding a safe haven is an equally compelling reason to get moving. The organizers of snail races have capitalized on this second motivator, giving birth to what has become a popular sport in France and the United Kingdom. For the World Snail Racing Championships, held in Conghan, England, pedigreed common garden snails are placed in the brightly lit center of a circle inscribed on damp cloth. At the command of "ready, set, slow!" the racing snails head for what they presume will be a less vulnerable spot: the finish line at the circle's outer perimeter, some 13 inches (33 cm) away.

Because the snails seldom take the most direct route, instead choosing a meandering path with numerous switchbacks and self-correcting U-turns, it's been difficult for race aficionados to calculate their peak speeds. Nonetheless, the 1998 edition of the *Guinness Book of World Records* awarded the top speed prize to a galloping gastropod named Archie, owned by Carl Branhorn of Pott Row, England. Archie completed the Conghan course in 2 minutes and 20 seconds. That's 28.3 feet (71.1 cm), or .005 miles per hour—not exactly a mad dash, but still well-deserving of a life in semi-retirement, serving as both the sire and the brood mare for future generations of racing snails.

FLEE OR BE EATEN

Predator avoidance appears to provide an even greater reason to get going, at least for snails in the oceans intertidal zones. The purple topshell (*Gibbula umbilicalis*), a common resident of Britain's seacoast, has been clocked at .045 miles (0.065 km) per hour while evading a predatory *Asterias rubens* starfish. That's still a crawl compared to a giant tortoise, which can travel at 0.17 miles (0.27 km) per hour, but considerably quicker than the Giant African land snail's record of 0.04 miles per hour.

If any snail species deserves a *Guinness Book* record for speed, the 0.6-inch-tall (15 mm) purple topshell would probably be it. Incidentally, the world's fastest mollusks are squids, which propel themselves by squirting jets of water through a siphon to attain speeds of about 25 miles (40 km) per hour.

Slime

As you watch a snail or slug move across a flat surface, you can't miss the silvery trail of slime left in its wake. The slime comes from special secretory cells in the animal's pedal gland, a large funnel-shaped opening at the front of the foot (right beneath the head), and from similar cells in the sole. More politely described as mucus, this slime plays a crucial role in the animal's efforts at mobility, simultaneously increasing traction and greasing the skids, as it were.

To get around, a snail or slug surfs on this layer of slime, propelling itself with waves of contracting muscle fibers in the animal's sole. To see the muscle fibers in action, place a snail on a piece of plate glass, let it settle for a few minutes, and watch it from beneath the glass. As the animal creeps across the smooth surface, you'll see a rippling pattern of alternating dark- and light-colored bands running the length of the sole, flowing in waves from the tail to the head. Should it come to a halt, the waves will stop until the snail resumes its forward or sideways progress.

Those light and dark bands represent oblique muscle fibers, relaxing and contracting in what are technically known as pedal waves. There are actually two sets of these muscle fibers, each performing separate chores. To move forward, one set—those fibers directed inward and rearward—contracts between waves, pulling the slug from the front and pushing off toward the back. Simultaneously, the second set—the fibers directed inward and forward— pulls the outer surface of the sole forward, generating each pedal wave. In some of the larger species, this second set of muscle fibers can generate as many as 18 waves at a time— quite an interesting show when viewed from below.

CONTROLLED CRAWLING

Individual control of all those muscle sets enables slugs or snails to slide along the edges of razor blades or crawl across crushed glass. To test what could very easily have been an old wives' tale, passed down from one gullible nature writer to the next, a test was mounted, using my own pet banana slugs, Chiquita and Dole, as gastropod guinea pigs. A razor blade was held between thumb and index finger, and one of the slugs was placed on the back of the hand. After tilting the hand to a 45-degree angle, the slug was prodded from behind, thus encouraging it to creep to higher ground, directly across the blade's edge.

The intrepid mollusk slid halfway across the blade, and then, as if losing interest in whatever lay ahead, made a U-turn with its body and slid back across the same cutting edge without a moment's pause.

STICKY OR SLICK

What you can't see, however, are the subtle changes to the mucus that occur with each wave of muscle contractions. External forces influence the chemical properties of mucus, so that it becomes more viscous (that is, less sticky) when pressure is applied, and less viscous (more sticky) when the pressure is released. Thus, the pressure of the leading edge of each wave liquefies the mucus, allowing the wave to pass through the slime with ease. The mucus

AFTER EXPLORING a range of alternatives to snail slime, including peanut butter and hair gel, engineers from Massachusetts Institute of Technology and the Catholic University of Leuven, Belgium, determined that mucus was not required for wall-climbing robots to operate. "We can make our own adhesive locomotion material with commercial products instead of harvesting slime from a snail farm," said MIT's Randy Ewoldt to a reporter from *Science Daily* in 2007.

gets stickier as the wave passes, and the slug can pull itself forward with a ratchet-like effect.

By capitalizing on the slime's sticky-making properties, resting snails and slugs can remain attached to a rock wall or other vertical surface, despite what one would assume to be the natural tendency of any slime-coated creature to slowly slide downhill to the ground.

MELTING SNAILS?

As a snail which melteth,
let every one of them pass away.

—PSALMS 58:8

This puzzling line in the Bible refers to the ancient belief that the slime trail made by a snail was subtracted from the substance of its body. In consequence, the farther it crept, the smaller the snail became, until it eventually wasted away into nothingness.

The Talmud also refers to this misunderstood phenomenon. It speaks of the *shablul* (Hebrew for snail) as "a creeping thing: when it comes out of its shell, saliva pours from itself, until it becomes liquid, and so it dies."

DARWIN ON SLIME

Most people are familiar with Charles Darwin for his theory of evolution, put forth in the book *On the Origin of Species*. Few are aware that the English scientist devoted years to the study of invertebrates, notably barnacles and earthworms. In his 1871 book, *The Descent of Man and Selection in Relation to Sex*, Darwin reported on the pulmonate predisposition for slime tracking:

> *An accurate observer, Mr. Lonsdale, informs me that he placed a pair of land snails (Helix pomatia), one of which was weakly, into a small and ill-provided garden. After a short time, the strong and healthy individual disappeared and was traced by its track of slime over a wall into an adjoining well-stocked garden. Mr. Lonsdale concluded that it had deserted its sickly mate; but after an absence of twenty-four hours it returned and apparently communicated the result of its successful exploration, for both then started along the same track and disappeared over the wall.*

MORE MARVELS OF MUCUS

With slugs, it's is not just the sole that can leave a slime trail. Virtually the entire body surface produces mucus—the mantle, the area surrounding the pneumostome, a

*Like something out of Cirque du Soleil, giant gardenslugs
can mate in midair, suspended by a silvery mucus thread.*

groove around the edge of the foot, the head, and, in some
species, the caudal gland at the base of the tail.

Although mucus unquestionably makes it easier for
slugs and snails to get around, scientists have determined
that mobility is not wholly dependent on it. Slugs with

their slime-producing glands cauterized can still move forward, although not as effectively as before.

Different kinds of mucus are used for self-defense, moisture control, and mating. When threatened, most slugs secrete an especially thick coating, making them harder to grasp. This thick mucus can gum up the works, actually sealing the mouths of snakes or shrews or causing larger predators such as ducks or dogs to gag.

The banana slug can suspend itself from a slender but strong slime cord, slowly lowering its body headfirst from the branches of trees or shrubs to reach the ground. The giant gardenslug employs a similar mucous thread to mate in midair. (Note to readers: do *not* try this at home.)

MUCOUS MAPS

Snails and slugs also seem to use mucus for navigation, employing their keen senses of smell to follow the chemical constituents of slime trails. In this way, they can seek mates, stalk other slugs, or simply find their way home. The difference in chemical concentrations of such clues may be minute, but snails can read them with ease, even if the trail is a week old. Studies of slime trails left by marine snails and limpets in coastal habitats have shown that the half-life of these trails—the time it takes for half the slime to disappear from the shore—can vary from twelve to forty days. That's long enough for these gastropods to establish migratory corridors along the craggiest seacoasts.

According to researcher C. David Rollo, "A slug can find its own shelter from more than three feet away by following the odor of its droppings within the crevice and, perhaps, by the scent of a special slime it exudes while resting." One individually marked banana slug was observed leaving a hole in spring and returning to the same hole in autumn.

Stomach

From both anatomical and behavioral perspectives, it would appear that land snails and slugs were born to eat. Most of their active hours are spent seeking and devouring fungi, lichens, algae, the soft parts of plants, living and dead, both below and above ground, a few insects, animal feces, carrion, and . . . other snails and slugs.

All other activities seem to be secondary. Many land slugs consume several times their own body weight each day; with the adults of many commonly encountered slug species weighing-in at well over an ounce, the nightly feasting by these hungry heifers can put serious dents in vegetable patches and flower gardens. Land snails can be just as voracious and, in some instances, can collectively strip a sapling of its leaves in a matter of days.

FROM CROP TO CRAP

Naturally, a pulmonate's insides reflect this consuming passion. Filling a large part of the body cavity is an expandable sac called a crop, within which enzymes from paired salivary glands help break down the fiber-rich diet. Partially processed food enters a smaller pouch-like stomach, where hepatic enzymes from another set of glands turn the food into mush. The mush passes by the great digestive gland (or liver) and from there into a long, looped intestine, which, in most species, opens to the outside world via the anus, somewhere on the body's right side.

By the time waste leaves the animal, as much as 90 percent of its nutritive value has been assimilated. Slug and snail droppings are wrapped in (what else?) mucus, and make great plant food for nearby foliage—assuming any greenery remains once the slug or snail finishes its eleventh, twelfth, or twentieth meal of the day.

Rev. A. H. Cook, in *Mollusks and Brachiopods* (1895), wrote of the black arion (*Arion ater*) thusly:

> Although normally frugivorous, is unquestionably carnivorous as well, feeding on all sorts of animal matter, whether decaying, freshly killed or even in a living state. It is frequently noticed feeding on earthworms; kept in

THE SECRET WORLD OF SLUGS AND SNAILS

captivity, it will eat raw beef; it does not disdain the carcasses of its own dead brethren. . . . Indeed it would seem almost difficult to name anything which *Arion ater* will not eat. . . . A specimen kept two days in captivity was turned out on a newspaper, and commenced at once to devour it.

Note: Cook also told of an adult black arion that would eat Pear's soap, "although with reluctance."

THE RADULA REVEALED

How that food gets into the crop is another interesting story. To feed, a snail first extends its mouth, and then uses its jaw—a solid structure that drops like a guillotine—to latch onto a lichen, leaf, or whatever. Then with its *radula*, a ribbon-like body part unique to mollusks, it rasps at the plant material, slowly but surely reducing the leaves of your beloved hosta or primrose into a more easily digestible pulp. (On a quiet day, you can actually hear the clicking of those jaws clamping and rasping of radulas at work—quite possibly the only audible sounds that these placid grazers can make.) The pulp is passed back into the creature's esophagus, where it is mixed with saliva and mucus before flowing into the crop.

A brief description of a slug's or snail's radula—a cross between a bastard file and a chainsaw—sounds like something out of *Evil Dead II*. It is armed with as many as

27,000 sharp, backward-pointing teeth. Like sharks, snails and slugs routinely lose and replace their teeth, with new ones coming from the rear of the radula to fill the gaps. Because all that feeding can be physically wearing, some species replace up to five rows of teeth each day.

In predatory land slug species, some radular teeth are elongated, razor-sharp, and often hooked. In addition to slashing at prey, these teeth perform like grappling hooks, holding tight to the flesh of an earthworm or other live treat until it can be dispatched. Radulas are also employed in slug-to-slug combat. Carefully examine the backs and sides of the giant gardenslug and other more aggressive slug species and you may see tiny dueling scars, usually acquired during territorial disputes. Such hot-blooded behavior from a cold-blooded beast!

Senses

They may be sluggish, but no one can say slugs and snails are out of touch with their environments. Few creatures are so intimately connected to their surroundings. The soft bodies of slugs and snails can feel the vibrations of your footsteps as the moist ground conducts them. They can "smell" molecules of food and water and, in some instances, see the metabolic heat from other animals and the warmth of decaying plants.

Both slug and snail bodies are dotted with sensory cells for tasting, smelling, and reacting to light and darkness from all angles. As one might expect, these cells are most densely clustered around the mouth and tentacles and at several locations along the length of the foot. The animals' insides are also equipped with sense receptors. These minute internal monitors send signals to the slug's command module (a ring of nine large nerve ganglia surrounding the esophagus) to initiate or terminate feeding, breeding, and other behaviors.

The ganglia also process information from two pairs of tentacles—hollow muscular tubes, the larger of which are known colloquially as "horns." They can move telescopically, in or out, up or down, as the situation requires. These tentacles can operate independently, letting the slug or snail gather information from several directions at the

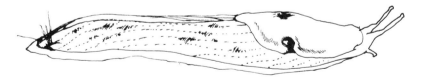

ARIOLIMAX COLUMBIANUS

Banana slugs gather sensory data from all angles, making them more aware of their surroundings than many other animals of Northwest coastal forests.

same time. It's this nifty parlor trick that has inspired the slang expression "snail-eyed"—an alcohol-induced state of double vision.

TOTALLY TUBULAR

The shorter pair of tubes is called sensory tentacles. Cast toward the ground, they help the slug sample its world at close range by smell and taste. The longer optic tentacles extend upward and are tipped with oval-shaped eyes, each fitted with a crude retina and lens. Although unable to perceive detailed images, these eyes can distinguish light from dark at a distance. One study of the milky slug revealed a second retina on each optic tentacle, possibly an infrared receptor for detecting and avoiding sources of heat.

IN THE DESCENT OF MAN, Darwin opined that the Gastropoda, "though capable of locomotion and furnished with imperfect eyes, do not appear to be empowered with sufficient mental powers for the members of the same sex to struggle together in rivalry, and thus, to acquire secondary sex characteristics. Nevertheless with the pulmoniferous gastropods, or landsnails, the pairing is preceded by courtship; for these animals, though hermaphrodites, are compelled by their structure to pair together."

Moral:
Learn from the Snail to
take reproof with patience,
And not put out your Horns
on all occasions.

—HILAIRE BELLOC,
A Moral Alphabet (1899)

SLUG AND SNAIL SMARTS

How smart are land snails and slugs? Measuring the intellectual capabilities of people is difficult enough; it is even more challenging to compare the intelligences of two different animal groups. In general, people rank the relative intelligence of animals by how closely the animals' behavior matches their own. In so doing, they overlook the fact that every species possesses the necessary brainpower to excel on its own terms. Perhaps it is safest to say that land snails are the best at being land snails . . . and leave it at that.

Personal experience has shown that the pulmonates are less hard-wired in their responses and, unlike insects, won't repeatedly bang against window screen while attempting to escape from a house. But are they actual problem solvers that can rely on memory to help them make wise choices? Laboratory studies suggest the answer to this question is yes.

SCENT SENSE

In one experiment, Canadian scientists Roger Croll and Ronald Chase tested the brainpower of East African land snails. Two groups of six snails each were fed either cucumbers or carrots for eighty-six days. Then they fasted for nine days before being tested for food preference in a special Y-shaped plexiglas olfactometer. The snails were released one at a time in the straight part of the device, while two streams of air—one smelling of carrots and the other of cucumber—flowed toward them.

The results were predictable, but impressive: each group oriented preferentially toward the odor of the food it had previously eaten. After this first experience with the olfactometer, the snails were fed lettuce for four days, put on a water-only diet for nine days, and tested again. This same experiment was repeated at two-week intervals, for a total of 120 days. Analysis of the data from these tests showed that the African snails continued to follow the odor of the food on which they had initially sated themselves—four months in the past!

Sex

All pulmonate mollusks are hermaphroditic, with each animal equipped with both male and female reproductive organs. For Mother Nature, this is the next best thing to Match.com for guaranteeing reproductive success among slow-moving and oftentimes geographically distanced members of the same species.

Hermaphroditism also means that, given no other choices, an adult slug or snail can mate with itself. Nonetheless, given an option, these animals will seek partners with which to trade genetic materials. By favoring the passage of chromosomes from both parents to the offspring, they nurture a healthier pool of pulmonate genes.

Lest you think that slugs and snails are promiscuous in their pairings, it should be mentioned that the actual one- or two-way exchange of sperm is preceded by an elaborate courtship ritual, which, along with the remarkable variation of genital shapes and sizes (supporting the lock-and-key hypothesis) supposedly reduces the chances of two individuals of separate species mating and giving rise to hybrids.

The love life of some snails
is confusing to Freudians.

—THOMAS R. HENRY,
The Strangest Things in the World (c. 1958)

SHALL WE DANCE?

During courtship, two slugs will circle each other, often for hours, with both partners engaged in ritualized bouts of lunging, nipping, and sideswiping with their tails. The two slugs may also display their disproportionately large sex organs. The giant gardenslug's penis is nearly half its total body length. In fact, penis size is reflected in the scientific name of one banana slug species: *dolichophallus*—Latin for "long penis."

"The sight of a courting pair of slugs majestically circling one another and ceremoniously rasping each other's flanks while they solemnly wave their enormous penises overhead puts the most improbably athletic couples of Pompeii and Khajuraho into a more appropriate and severely diminished perspective," note researchers C. David Rollo and William G. Wellington. "Athletic" is an even more appropriate adjective for great gray garden slugs, which are able to copulate in midair, suspended by stretchy strands of mucus up to 17¾ inches (45 cm) long.

As courtship progresses, a banana slug pair intertwines, wrapping themselves in an "S" position and stimulating each other for several more hours. Their genital areas (immediately in front of the pneumostome) swell as the pair moves even closer together. Penetration takes place, then each slug alternately releases and receives sperm.

A MATING MYSTERY

But in the case of the banana slug, that's hardly the end of this amazing routine. Now the slugs must disengage— a challenge for two animals so amply endowed and thoroughly covered in sticky mucus. After long bouts of writhing and pulling, the pair may resort to what scientists call *apophallation*. Presented in more familiar terms, this means that one slug gnaws off the penis of the other.

Is there an advantage to such odd behavior? Yes, according to Adrian Forsyth, author of *A Natural History of Sex*. The apophallated slug, says Forsyth, "cannot regrow his penis and is now obligated to be a female and forced to offer eggs. It may be that the castrator can raise his reproductive success by increasing locally the density of females."

Slug scientist Albert Mead has suggested that apophallation may be nature's way of maintaining the species. After all, he explains, in other animal species, such as the tusk-intensive wooly mammoth and heavily antlered Irish elk, gigantism has been a precursor to extinction. Only by submitting to the shears can banana slugs maintain their inordinate organs.

It's a nice thought, but few of Mead's peers have taken this second hypothesis seriously. In fact, a preponderance of evidence suggests that many banana slugs are born with a hemiphallic condition, where the male genitalia are reduced but not absent. In a sample of over 400 banana slugs collected on Hog Island in Tomales Bay, California, all were hemiphallic. "It seems unlikely that the entire population of a perennial species would consist of juveniles," notes Barry Roth in his article in a 2004 issue of *The Veliger*. "But it is plausible that an isolated population on a small island could be monomorphic for one state of a genital polymorphism, whether from founder effect or . . . from conditions that favored an extreme ratio of hemiphallic individuals."

According to slug expert Janet L. Leonard, a professor of biology at UC Santa Cruz, apophallation has been observed in about 5 of 100 banana slug specimens. However, cases where the slug's penis is reduced or entirely absent are considerably more common, suggesting that the ability to mate without outside help—a condition Leonard calls "selfing"—has its benefits. Let's say the breeding season is foreshortened because of a drought or other adverse environmental conditions. Should this happen, it may become advantageous for a slug to "self" rather than refrain from mating and, as a result, leave no offspring to carry the slug's genetic legacy once the environment returns to a more slug-friendly state. Energetically speaking, "once a population starts to 'self,' a penis becomes an expense, not a benefit," Leonard says.

A GAME OF DARTS

The elaborate sex lives of slugs are well matched by the pre-coital games played by land snails. When the paths of two mature brown gardensnails cross, the pair will touch tentacles, and then rise up on their soles until their mouths come in contact. This leads to a "kiss" that lasts for a minute or two. Next, the snails reposition themselves, bowing slightly to mouth one another's genitals. The next step, about 30 minutes into this ritual, involves mutual stimulation of the genital areas. Now it's time . . . to play darts.

Well, not exactly. The *Helix* snails and several other related species carry one or more love darts in a muscular internal chamber. Made of pure calcium carbonate, with lateral vanes and a sharp point, the dart is designed to penetrate a sex partner's skin. Scholars once believed that such darts were calcium-laden nuptial gifts—in a snail's world, the equivalent of a box of chocolates or an engagement ring. Others thought the dart was fired to arouse the receiver while indicating the shooter's readiness to get it on.

IN THE FRENCH DOCUMENTARY *MICROCOSMOS*, two *Helix* snails are filmed *en flagrante*, enthusiastically engaged in the business of making babies to an operatic composition, *Le Peuple de l'Herbe* (The People of the Grass), sung by mezzo-soprano Mari Kobayashi.

Nowadays, the dart's function is better understood for what it is: a tool of male manipulation. Each dart contains a kind of mucus that causes the recipient's female reproductive duct to temporarily contract, shortening the distance that sperm must travel before reaching the chamber where the eggs are stored. Without the dart's help in preparing the way, many sperm cells fail to reach the storage area, and instead are digested en route.

According to Ronald Chase, professor emeritus at McGill University in Montreal, being hit with a love dart increases the chances of fertilization but is not wholly necessary for copulatory success. "Poor shooting is commonplace—one third of all love darts either fail to penetrate the skin or they miss the target completely," he told a reporter from the *McGill Tribune*.

The ancient Greeks' knowledge of snail love darts may have inspired the many myths in which mortals are struck by Cupid's arrows, kindling the flames of love within. The connection seemed obvious to Chase, who went so far as to hire a grad student to trace any depictions of Cupid or his cosmic mother, Aphrodite, in the presence of snails. The search yielded nothing, not even a pottery shard, to substantiate Chase's belief. But as they say, absence of evidence is not necessarily evidence of an absence. In other words, stay tuned.

A FEW KINDS OF SNAILS, among them the mountain-snails (genus *Oreohelix*) of the Rocky Mountains and Great Basin, are egg-retainers. They hold their fertilized eggs in a uterus of sorts, where the babies develop into tiny snails that, at birth, crawl out of the uterus, and go for a stroll without any assistance from mom or dad.

SNAIL EGGS

Admittedly, such pulmonate push-and-pull seems bizarre by our standards. In this light, one might be surprised to learn that snail egg laying is no more extraordinary than that of a chicken. Transparent, golden, or pearly-white

HELIX LAYING EGGS

A clutch of Helix snail eggs can contain an average of eighty-five individuals, each waiting to hatch and get on with its life.

round or oval-shaped eggs are deposited in clutches of anywhere from thirty to fifty, usually beneath a piece of wood or debris or in a small crevice or hole in the ground. Banana slugs seldom lay more than forty eggs at a time, but the brown gardensnail and several other species can lay larger numbers with greater frequency, so that individuals may deposit as many as five hundred fertile eggs in a year.

Depending on weather and soil conditions (slugs and snails will not lay their eggs when water saturation in the soil is below 10 percent), eggs hatch in three to eight weeks. Eggs that are laid in late autumn usually over-winter and hatch the next spring. The hatchlings look like miniature adults, but lack the defense mechanisms of their parents and wear shells that are thin and frail, so they are extremely vulnerable to predators. They grow quickly, however, and move beyond this dangerous stage after a few months. By the end of a season, they are often indistinguishable from their parents.

Sleep

Slugs and snails can sleep for hours, days, weeks, and months. If ambient conditions are right, they can enter into prolonged states of slumber that may last for several years.

The technical terms for these prolonged sleepy states is either hibernation (the near cessation of body functions in response to extreme cold) or aestivation (similar, but brought about by extreme heat and dryness). The former tactic is employed by bears and many other mammals in far northern climes. The latter is especially advantageous for amphibians and fish in sun-drenched realms. (The fact that toads may survive for several seasons within hardened clumps of mud may have engendered the medieval belief that these animals were created parthenogenetically by farmers' spades striking certain "rocks.")

OBLOMOVISTIC WAYS

Both of these behaviors are collectively referred to as Oblomovism—a word borrowed from novelist Ivan Goncharov and his portrait of Russian nobleman Ilya Oblomov, known for his arrant laziness. Employing their Oblomovistic powers to the fullest, the two *Helix* snail species can remain dormant throughout the cold months of late fall and winter and again in the hottest days of summer and fall. Snug in their epiphragm-covered shells, these snails can sleep for periods of five or six months at a time. However, such lengthy snoozes might seem like mere catnaps to several desert-dwelling snail species, according to malacologist Robert Stearns.

In his paper "On the Vitality of Certain Land Molluscs," Stearns told of one dry-land inhabitant, collected at the southern tip of Mexico's Baja Peninsula. After keeping nine of these sealed-off snails in a box, the scientist awakened them with moistened chickweed and "other tender vegetable food," two years, two months, and sixteen days after they had been taken from their desert habitat. Even more impressive was Stearns's story of a specimen of *Helix veitchii* that lived from 1859 to 1865, a period of six years, in a similar suspended state.

Can you top that? Stearns could. His paper also described an Oblomovistic *Helix desertorum*, the Egyptian "Snail of the Desert," that spent nearly four years in the British Museum, glued to a tablet inside a glass display case, before workers discovered this sound-sleeping snail was still alive and released it.

PERCHANCE TO DREAM

Thus, while we can agree that land snails are world-champion sleepers, it has yet to be established if these mollusks can dream. If they can, one wonders whether such dreams include nightmares, in which the dreamers are being chased by garter snakes or standing shell-less before their peers.

The world authority on the interpretation of dreams, psychiatrist Carl Jung believed that, in the enigmatic inner language of dreams, the snail represents the self. Other psychoanalysts maintain that the snail's shell symbolizes the conscious mind and its maker, the unconscious state. It's no coincidence that the logo of C. G. Jung Institute of San Francisco features the silhouettes of four snails traveling in a circle around a center point. According to the Institute, "the broad foot of the snail is sensation and its antennae are intuition." The logo has often been invoked as "a sign of our swift-moving and decisive organizational style," the Institute wryly concedes.

SLEEP STUDIES

Although we know the environmental conditions that compel snails to "hit the mattress," the factors that rouse them from their slumbers remain unclear. One research team investigated the influence of moist air, placing groups of 48 snails in enclosures and exposing them to different relative humidities. If the relative humidity was less than 58 percent, most of the snails remained dormant, while those in chambers with 74 percent relative humidity became active. However, the results of this experiment could not be reproduced: identical conditions were insufficient in re-awakening most of the snails after their earlier nap.

The same team looked at the effects of air temperature on sleeping snails. By exposing Oblomovistic snails to air temperatures ranging from 41–91 degrees Fahrenheit (5–33°C), they learned that the majority awakened at lower temperatures. Darkness also proved to be a factor: the snails were more likely to arise after long periods of being kept in the dark.

Let's see now . . . where would sleeping snails find warm, moist air, and lack of light? If you answered "a garden at night," proceed directly to page 121 for information on slug and snail control.

Shell

Finding an unoccupied snail shell while gardening is an invitation to pause, put down that trowel or pruners, and contemplate the object's departed maker. That such a flawless form, with its subtly etched patterns and arresting mathematical asymmetry, could be built by a quiet encroacher on our cultivated beds is a mind-stretching paradox—a Zen koan of sorts. Similar shells have inspired poets, architects, philosophers, and fine artists alike. The graceful turns of El Caracole, the circular stargazing observatory at the Mayan city of Chichen Itza, and the breathtaking forms of contemporary glass blower

Dale Chihuly's seashell series have been informed by the workings of the lowly land snail.

A snail's shell is made of calcium carbonate crystals. Snail blood contains high concentrations of this near-ubiquitous salt in a liquid form. The dissolved compound is further concentrated within the tissue of the mantle and secreted, along with a brownish organic material called *conchiolin*, to make a new layer of shell.

Outside the mantle, the liquid calcium carbonate becomes crystallized. It is laid down in overlapping layers within the concholin, forming a laminate, much like the layers of chitin in a crab's or a lobster's shell, but with even greater material strength. In land snails, this laminate is known as *aragonite*. The second most common form of calcium carbonate on our planet, it is found not only in mollusk shells, but in rocks from the sea floor, concretions in geysers and hot springs, and stalactites from Carlsbad Caverns and other large limestone caves.

A PERIOSTRACUM FOR ALL SEASONS

Despite its superior properties, this rugged laminate is still vulnerable to outside effects. Like our own calcium-rich teeth, the hard shell can be gradually worn down, either from contact with even harder rocks and minerals in the soil, or by the properties of tannic acids in decaying leaf litter. In addition, a range of so-called bioeroders (certain kinds algae, fungi, worms, and other small, non-predatory organisms) may assault the shell, digging tunnels or pits in its exposed surfaces. To overcome these challenges, land snail shells are often covered by a *periostracum*—a varnish-like layer of protein that shields the mineral-rich layers below. The periostracum may also sport numerous small hairs to discourage bioeroders from getting attached. In some land snail species, including the Oregon forestsnail, the periostracum can become worn down with age; older specimens may have "bald spots" where the chalky white calcium carbonate layer is easy to see.

WHORL OF COLOR

The patterns of bands of contrasting colors on land snail shells are produced by color-depositing cells located along the edge of the mantle. These cells get their colors natu-rally, from the *carotenoids* (yellow/orange pigments), *mela-nins* (black to tan pigments), and *porphyrins* (red pigments) in foods the snails eat. Although most of these color cells are stationary, some migrate along the mantle while secreting pigments—an activity that yields patterns of oblique stripes—as opposed to broad unvarying bands—within the shell.

For land snails, the process of shell making begins before birth. The fragile rudiments of a shell are secreted by the embryonic snail's mantle while the little upstart is still in the egg. Upon hatching, this small sliver of shell becomes the apex of the spiral on which subsequent whorls are added. With each whorl, the shell grows exponentially larger, giving its fabricator more room for growth as well. Much of the snail's body is confined to the most recently produced whorl, with the digestive and reproductive glands occupying earlier whorls. The snail is unable to move freely in or out of this protective tube.

> *In a collection of shells which came from France some years ago, I found several snails of different colors which were joined one to the other. The collector had cut the top from an empty brown snail and placed a living snail with a yellow shell upon it, tying the two together. The snail, supposing that its shell had been broken, immediately began to repair the wound, and closed up the breach with its shell-secreting mantle, so that the two shells became one.*
>
> —CHARLES FREDRICK HOLDER,
> *Half Hours with the Lower Animals* (c. 1905)

Spread

Charles Darwin's trip to the Galapagos Islands aboard the HMS *Beagle* in the fall of 1835 showed the inquisitive ship's naturalist an important aspect of evolutionary theory. Separated from the mainland of Ecuador by miles of ocean, many Galapagos animals and plants had gradually morphed into new species, unable to breed with their mainland relatives. From this, Darwin reasoned that isolation—the separation of populations by geological or other barriers—could play a strong part in the process of creating new species.

The stay-at-home lifestyles of land slugs and snails, coupled with the proverbial "snail's pace" with which they move from place to place, make these invertebrates among the most physically isolated forms of animate nature. Because isolated populations will evolve independently, it should come as no surprise that there are thousands of land snail species worldwide.

THE GREAT DIVIDE

Mountain ranges are insurmountable barriers to pulmonates and, even with Kobashi Issa's poetic encouragement, a snail isn't likely to climb Mount Fuji, however slowly, on its own. For this reason, the indigenous land snail faunas of western and eastern North America are fundamentally different, forever separated by the Rockies, the Cascades, the Sierras, and a few other ranges.

Islands are also major shapers of speciation. On the Hawaiian island of O'ahu, one can readily see the effects of isolation among populations of the native tree snail *Achatinella*. Separated by a series of steep slopes, the snails of this genus in five neighboring valleys have diverged into five separate species, each with distinctive markings. Tree snails from the valley of Niu (species: *A. fulgens*) have white shells with several brown bands, whereas shells of snails from Palolo (species: *A. fuscobesis*) are white with only one brown band. Shells from Manoa (species: *A. stewartii*) are golden with single white bands, whereas in nearby Aiea, the tree snail *A. turgida*'s golden shell lacks bands altogether. In Wailupe, midway between Niu and Palolo, shells of the tree snail *A. cestus* are neither white nor gold; they are uniquely marked with brown striations. Now that your head is spinning, consider this: there are more than forty recognized species of *Achatinella* tree snails endemic to the island of O'ahu, all of which are listed as endangered under the federal Endangered Species Act.

The Reverend H. G. Barnacle, a British missionary-naturalist, shared his experiences with tree snails in Hawaii: "When up in the mountains of O'ahu, I heard the grandest but wildest as from hundreds of Aeolean harps wafted to me by the breeze and a native told me it came from singing shells. It was sublime. I could not believe it, but a tree close at hand proved it. Upon it were thousands of the snails. The animals drew after their shells which grated against the wood and so caused the sounds. The multitude of sounds produced the fanciful music."

SNAILS FROM ABOVE

How land snails and slugs arrived in Hawaii and other islands is no less astonishing. It turns out that birds carry small pulmonates and their sticky eggs attached to their plumage. One study, conducted in 1965, recovered land snails—as few as one and as many as ten—from the feathers of seven different species of birds. In another 1960s study, this time of ninety-six woodcocks during their migration, researchers determined that eleven of the birds were carrying an average of three snails apiece.

The likeliest agents in the Hawaiian transfer were oceanic birds, such as petrels and terns. Several species of petrels nest in burrows, dug in the moist, peaty, and, possibly, snail-laden soil of remote islands. It's thought that the snails attach themselves to the down of petrel chicks, which, even after fledging, are still adorned with bits of the fluffy stuff. When the young petrels take to the air, snails and their eggs get free trips to distant lands, sometimes more than a thousand miles away. At journey's end, the birds shake off the snails and eggs, leaving them to become established and speciate in their microcosmic world. This strategy works best for small snails; large snails may have reached the islands by clinging to driftwood rafts and, at the mercy of weather and tides, subjecting themselves to the wind, rain, and salt spray for several weeks.

Weather has wholly aided and abetted the spread of snails and slugs. Over the years, there have been reports of periodic showers of snails, apparently after these lightweight animals were sucked up by tornadoes and deposited in rain-clouds. One of the most notable snail showers took place in 1886 in the English town of Redruth, where afterwards, land snails were collected from roads and fields by the hat-ful. A similar incident supposedly occurred in Bristol, according to the *Philosphical Magazine* of 1878. Here, the snails fell in such numbers that they had to be shoveled up.

> *When I slip, just lightly, in the dark,*
> *I know it isn't a wet leaf,*
> *But you, loose toe from the old life,*
> *The cold slime come into being,*
> *A fat, five-inch appendage*
> *Creeping slowly over the wet grass,*
> *Eating the heart out of my garden.*

> —THEODORE ROETHKE,
> *Words for the Wind* (c. 1981)

Life-Saving Secrets
in Slug Slime

The mucous-secreting cells of the banana slug are enormous; about a half a millimeter long, they can be seen with the naked eye. This attribute makes these animals superb specimens for scientists studying the mechanics of mucus production and of mucus itself.

In the 1990s, University of Washington professor emeritus Ingrith Deyrup Olsen kept several dozen of these gargantuan gastropods, plucked from the isolated terrain of Tatoosh Island, the northernmost piece of property in the conterminous United States. To meet the slugs' needs for a cool, moist clime, Deyrup Olsen kept her spineless treasures, the invertebrate equivalents of laboratory rats and mice, in a walk-in cooler on the UW campus. Her research assistants fed them mixed greens and lovingly spritzed them with plant misters.

"Mucus is a tremendously important protective agent for any cell—from a slug, a human or any other living creature—that comes in contact with the environment," Deyrup Olsen told readers of *Current Science* magazine. "It's a very complex material, and we don't fully understand its function in any organism."

After many years of independent study, Deyrup Olsen teamed up with UW biochemist Pedro Verdugo, to put the secrets of banana slug slime to good use—as a mechanism for delivering mega-doses of cancer-fighting chemicals to sites of affliction within the human body. Because cancer medicines are extremely toxic to healthy and harmful cells alike, it's essential for each dose to hit only the target—a tumor, for example—while leaving the rest of the cells alone. The larger the dose that can be delivered to the site, the better.

That's where banana slug slime comes in. Inside the slugs' cells are tiny secretory granules—unique storage containers for holding and releasing mucus-producing material on demand. The material in each granule is a polymer gel, composed of long chains of molecules that are neither liquid nor solid but somewhere in-between. The gel can move from a highly packed, condensed state to a more fluid, expanded state as conditions inside and outside the cell change.

To produce mucus, a slug's secretory cells release the polymer gel material. Outside the cell, the material comes in contact with water molecules . . . and presto! The polymer gel grabs onto every available water molecule, swelling rapidly in the process to 30 times its previous size in about six seconds. It's a nifty trick: if all this water-grabbing activity took place within the cell, the rapid expansion would cause the slug's secretory cells to burst.

The gel's remarkably hydrophilic properties make pulmonate slime nearly impossible to wash off. Most gardeners have learned the hard way that rubbing their hands under running water only makes matters worse: a little slime soon becomes a lot. Rather, the slime should be wiped off with a dry towel *before* washing. An alternative clean-up strategy involves rubbing one's dry hands together, as if removing rubber cement, to form a gummy ball that can now be tossed into the trash.

Armed with his knowledge of slime mechanics, Verdugo and Deyrup Olsen developed a synthetic polymer gel. Loaded with a cancer-fighting drug, the gel can be crammed inside a synthetic liposome (a droplet of fat) and injected into a cancer patient's body. Carried by blood to the disease site, the gel comes into contact with the body's fluids and quickly expands. Such expansion breaks the liposome, delivering a much bigger and more powerful dose of the drug than was previously achievable.

CHAPTER IV

Sharing Our Gardens: Coexisting with Slugs and Snails

*Neither man nor any animal can
afford triumph . . . completely.*

—JOSEPH WOOD KRUTCH

Let's face it: you probably won't be able to eliminate every slug and snail in your garden. A British zoologist proved the sheer impossibility of this objective after he systematically removed four hundred slugs from a quarter-acre garden every night for several years without reducing the garden's resident populations. In a second case, researchers in England collected slug samples forty-one, fifty-eight, fifty-three, and forty-six times in successive years. Annually, between 10,000 and 17,000 slugs were gathered, yet there was no appreciable dip in the gastropod fauna of that garden site.

And who would want to get rid of every slug or snail? Whether on land or at sea, slugs and snails are small but precious cogs in nature's Grande Machine. Native pulmonate mollusks were here long before we arrived on the scene, so, ethically speaking, they have just as much of the right, if not more, to blaze their own silver-lined trails through the wilderness. Unfortunately, the paths of most non-native pulmonates often lead to our best bib lettuce or Thai basil plants. Equally unfortunate is the tendency of many gardeners to place blame on all slugs and snails, including the more benign woodland species, for the damage done by non-native despoilers.

The challenge for most gardeners is to maintain a balance—a concept, alas, that the non-native slugs and snails seem to know nothing about. That balancing act can be difficult for people, too. Most of us feed, water, and weed our gardens for maximum yield. Because of our horticultural prowess, there is seldom a real shortage of food for the slithering hordes.

Knowing When (and How) to Act

Maintaining a balance means knowing when things have gotten out of hand. And having a few slugs and snails in your beds and borders does not qualify as an infestation, nor does it justify extreme measures. Explore what the experts call your "acceptable level of aesthetic injury"—in other words, how many of these gastropods can you tolerate before drawing a line in the sand? Can a meaningful and lasting peace be forged between man and mollusk? If, after some introspection, you decide to take action, at the very least try the most humane and least environmentally damaging controls first. Responsible methods of slug and snail control are presented in the sections that follow. Ready, set, go.

ALTER THE ENVIRONMENT

The most effective and least destructive form of control is to make your lands less hospitable for slugs and snails. This may involve selecting plants such as rhododendrons and other hard-leaved evergreens that do not appeal to the pulmonate palate. At the same time, one should avoid those trees, shrubs, and groundcovers that snails and slugs actively seek (for examples of both types of plants, turn to pages 127–128). Next, rid the garden of ornamental driftwood, rotting logs, and any statuary, flagstone, bricks, or pavers. In so doing, you will eliminate most of the best places for gastropods and gardeners to play hide-and-seek.

Switch the watering regime from dusk, when slugs and snails are most active, to dawn, when the light-shunning majority is knocking off for the day. Be frugal with water supplies; instead of wetting down entire surfaces, aim sprinklers and sprayers to hit only the foliage and deny any thirsty snails and slugs.

Most pulmonates lay eggs in heavy soils that, by retaining moisture, prevent the eggshells of their offspring from drying out and cracking. To limit egg laying, make sure that any wet ground is well drained. Add sand or coarse grit, along with well-rotted manure or compost, to improve soil drainage. In so doing, you are making the subterranean scene less appealing, especially to burrowing slug species. The extra height of raised beds can also improve soil drainage. In summer and early fall, rake up the first several inches of soil, exposing any eggs to the dry air and inviting insects and birds to eat them.

Some gardeners lure pest slugs and snails away from their prized garden foliage with plantings of horseradish, mustards, marigolds, or other greenery with high gastropod appeal. By regularly checking this sacrificial vegetation, one can take the browsers out of the gene pool. There's always a chance that the pests might consider these plants appetizers and, after snacking on them, will begin to comb the rest of the garden for whatever will comprise the main course. To discourage such foraging, keep the sacrificial plants far enough from vegetables or ornamentals that, for the hungry slugs and snails, all that back-and-forth travel becomes a bother.

There was a time when we thought we had a slug problem, they annoyed us so. However, we brought the problem under control more by changing our attitude than by controlling the slugs.

—BARBARA AND MORT MATHER,
Gardening for Independence (1977)

Plants Pulmonates Avoid Eating

Adapted from *The Complete Shade Gardener*
by George Schenk (Timber Press, Incorporated, 2002).

Agapanthus

Alocasia

Astilbe

Baby's tears

Bamboo

Bedding Begonias
(*Semperflorens*)

Begonia "Cleopatra"

Bleeding heart

Bromeliads

Campanula poscharskya

Coral bells

Cyclamen

Dichondria

Duchenesea

Endymion hispanicus

Epimedium (taller species)

Evergreen candy tuft

Ferns

Foxglove

Galium odoratum

Gaultheria

Hedychium

Imaptiens

Ivy

Juniper

Kenilworth ivy

Linnaea

London pride

Nandina

Oxalis oregona

Sanseveria

Sedum
(except *S. maximus*)

Sempervivum

Solomon's seal

Taxus

Thailictrum

Thymus serpyllium

Viola hederacea or
Rupestris

Wandering Jew

Plants Pulmonates Love to Eat

Adapted from *The Complete Shade Gardener*
by George Schenk (Timber Press, Incorporated, 2002).

Asarum	Lettuce
Athyrium niponicum "Pictum"	Lilies
Campanula carpatica, isophylla, and other low-growing forms	*Lobelia* (perennial)
	Parochetus communis
Doronicum	Primroses
Erythronium	Trillium
Gentians (autumn-flowering)	Tuberous begonias
	Viola sororia

BIOLOGICAL BARRIERS

Put impediments in the way of slugs' and snails' travel plans. In most situations, barring their passage has been proven to be a better solution than trying to eliminate all the land-dwelling snails and slugs after they've found the entryway to your Garden of Eden. Some gardeners say that maintaining rows of garlic or onion plants will act as gastropod deterrents. Others claim that paths of diatomaceous earth, wood ash, or shredded bark will impede forward motion by drying out and irritating the highly sensitive soles of slugs and snails. Alas, these deterrents work best under dry conditions at times when the ground-hugging gastropods are least likely to encounter such paths. And anyone who thinks the sharp edges of crushed gravel paths will deter slugs is wrong. If gravel is an inhibitor, it's because it dries more quickly than topsoil, to the dismay of moisture-loving slugs.

In England, Delphinium growers have reported success with aluminum sulfate crystals sprinkled on the ground between plants. The crystals act as irritants or promote dehydration in snails and slugs. In the United States, this chemical is frequently used to induce blue flowers on hydrangeas; however, no information on its effectiveness against slugs is available.

> Get up, sweet Slug-a-bed, and see
> The Dew bespangling Herbe and Tree.
>
> —ROBERT HERRICK,
> "Corinna's Going a-Maying" (1648)

MOTHER NATURE'S HELPERS

Gardeners can up the ante by inviting pulmonate-eating predators into their yards. Robins, crows, jays, and many other wild birds are known gastropod gastronomes, and making your garden bird-friendly increases the chances of becoming slug- or snail-free. Thrushes are recognized snail eaters, well known for their habit of using a stone or a paver as an anvil on which to break shells, liberating the raw escargot inside. Our domestic feathered friends also eat snails and slugs. However, the damage to plants from unsupervised chickens, geese, and swans can sometimes exceed that of the pulmonates. Purportedly, guinea hens and ducks are less damaging to gardens than other fowl, because they don't scratch as much.

GUINEA HENS

Guinea fowl are superb slug and snail catchers; their fertilized eggs and live keets (chicks) can be ordered from breeders by mail and reared to adulthood.

The much-maligned thrush, too, is a mighty hunter of Snails, and, in spite of its autumnal raids on the fruit, does such good service in Snail-killing before the world is astir, that it ought to be encouraged by the gardener, and the fruit which it eats considered as the wages paid for killing the Snail.

—THE REVEREND J. G. WOOD, M.A., F.L.S.,
The Illustrated Natural History (1863)

Snakes and lizards may not be the most popular creatures on the planet, but they excel at patrolling the garden and eating any small life forms they can catch. Frogs and toads are also good groundskeepers, especially the nocturnally active species. Because frogs are semi-aquatic, they require a pond or pool nearby. Toads, on the other hand, need less moisture, and are therefore more effective in rockeries and other, more arid, sectors of the garden.

Those fleet-footed black beetles people see while weeding are welcome allies in the War Against Slime. Collectively known as *carabids*, these wingless, six-legged hunters can easily outrun even the fastest land mollusk, cutting away with their sharp, sideways-moving jaws to inflict one or more lethal wounds. Having dispatched their prey, the beetles lap up the slug's or snail's body fluids while gnawing at the soft-bodied victim's flesh.

Three major genera of gastropod-eating carabids—the *Scaphinotus*, *Cychrus*, and *Sphaeroderus*—are native to the Pacific coastal states. Members of these genera have long legs, large bodies, and extremely narrow heads. Their narrow-headedness is an adaptation that allows them to eat snails while still in their shells.

> *To be truthful, although I have seen Scaphinotus eat a slug, I have never seen them eat the whole thing. Indeed, that could be a bit like trying to eat a whole elephant. And really, eating any part of a slug is just as good as eating the whole thing, don't you think, since it will surely die from the wound.*
>
> —LOUISE KULZER, *Scarabogram* (1997)

Tiger beetles of the genus Omus are also snail and slug predators, outpacing their prey with ease. A cousin of Omus, the Australian tiger beetle (Megacephala whelani) can hit a stride of 5.6 miles (9 km) per hour. If one of these speedsters were the size of a human, it would be racing in excess of 700 miles (1,127 km) per hour! Not nearly as speedy, woodland centipedes are nonetheless as valuable for removing pest slugs and the hatchlings of pest snails. Think twice before swatting at one of these much-maligned arthropods. You could be killing a good friend.

Unlike ladybugs and mantises, you can't buy carabids or tiger beetles at the garden store. But by increasing the habitat value of the land, one can entice these helpful insects into settling down and being of service. Leave a patch of native plants near the garden as a low-maintenance wildlife sanctuary for beetles. Encourage the growth of forest mosses, under which several carabid species are known to hide. And if you want the beetles' continued aid, avoid using pelleted slug baits, which can poison the carabids along with the targeted mollusks. In one laboratory study, carabid beetles more readily supped on slugs, both alive and dead, that had ingested the pulmonate-killing chemical metaldehyde. This preference for pesticide-tainted meat may be attributed to the reduction of anti-predatory traits in the mucus from the chemically compromised slugs.

When black snails on the road you see,
Then on them morrow rain will be.

—OLD ENGLISH RHYME

HANDPICKING

Handpicking slugs and snails from one's plants can be an effective control, especially at night, when these animals are most active. If you're squeamish about slime (and most people are), arm yourself with a long-handled dandelion digger or a pair of long tweezers. Plop any captives into a jar filled with soapy water, which will prevent them from sliding up the glass sides and slipping over the top. As an extra security measure, use a jar with a screw top, as slugs and snails have been known to push with sufficient force to pop the lid off of a yogurt container.

For severe infestations, recruit the neighborhood kids and offer a bounty for each slug they bring in. Remember to set a reasonable price, never more than a nickel. One Seattle gardener boasted of capturing as many as 800 slugs in one night; at 10 cents a head, he would be out 80 dollars!

Bill Symondson of the Cardiff School of Biosciences suggests making a slug spear, with a hatpin securely fastened to a stick, creating a tool similar to those used by park litter patrols. "Whereas a beer trap might catch a dozen or so slugs in a week, you can easily kill a couple of hundred an hour by searching," he writes. "If you don't mind remarks about your waning sanity, you can even mow the lawn at night," he suggests.

Regard the Snail
That in a narrow room
Inhabits both
His tower and his tomb.
His hollow house
Poised like a sculptured wave

Becomes at once
His fortress and his grave.

—JOSEPH AUSLANDER,
"The Snail" (1936)

TRAPPING SNAILS AND SLUGS

Either store-bought or built at home, slug and snail traps offer a more passive approach to pest control. One time-honored device is the beer trap. Little more than a shallow pan or saucer with its rim flush to the ground, it employs the scent of the brew's chief constituents, malt and yeast, in particular the volatile components acetoin, diacetyl, and dihydroxyacetone, to lure pulmonates to a watery grave.

Some of the best beer traps are made from plastic butter tubs or cottage cheese containers, the depth of which makes it harder for satiated slugs to escape. Cut a few one-inch-square (2.5-cm-square) doors into the sides of either vessel and use the lid to deflect rain, thus preventing dilution.

Although no single beer brand has been proved most effective at offing slugs, a 1997 study conducted by Whitney Cranshaw of Colorado State University concluded that Kingsbury Malt Beverage (produced by G. Heileman Brewing Company) was superior for attracting the grey fieldslug. The single wine tested—Gallo Pink

Chablis—proved unappealing to the same slugs and, to quote Cranshaw, "Fortification of flattened beer treatments with alcohol did not affect capture." It should be noted that, in Cranshaw's tests, slugs preferred Budweiser to PBR two to one.

Adding a dash of baker's yeast will make a beer trap more effective. A few pulmonate carcasses floating in the swill will also add to the lure of the trap, as many gastropods are not averse to feeding on their own kind. However, because the beer in these traps will eventually sour and lose its potency, it's important to keep a fresh supply on hand. Perhaps this is why so many gardeners are especially fond of beer traps. In lieu of beer, an equally potent attractant can be concocted from two tablespoons of flour, ½ teaspoon of brewer's yeast, and one teaspoon of sugar mixed in two cups of warm water.

A simple slug trap is easy to build and can be cleaned and recycled after many months of continuous use.

A very simple but rather gruesome trap consists of two boards, one on top of the other, separated by a few small stones. The trap is set at dusk and, in the morning, the stones are removed and the upper board is lowered with a few foot-stomps, crushing any slugs or snails that have sought sanctuary from the light of day. Other hungry pulmonates will be attracted by the mashed bodies, so this procedure can be repeated as often as one likes, over a succession of days, weeks, or months.

Other effective lures for shade-loving slugs and snails include grapefruit rinds turned dome-side up, 2-gallon (7.5-l) flowerpots (whose insides serve as slug and snail collectors, or plastic lawn or leaf bags strategically placed on the soil's surface. These lures should be checked first thing in the morning, before rising temperatures and reduced humidity force the inhabitants to seek other shelters.

A more refined trap, euphemistically called a slug hotel, can be built from an empty plastic soda pop bottle. Cut the bottle at its shoulder, just before it starts to taper toward the neck. Stick the piece you have just cut off into the bottle, neck-first. Tape the two pieces together with duct or electrical tape. Fill the trap half full with beer or apple cider and bury it sideways in your garden, so that the entrance is level with the ground. When your hotel is fully occupied, untape the top and empty its contents into your garbage can or compost bin. Refill it with beer or cider and post a "vacancy" sign.

KATY, BAR THE DOOR

Structural barriers may be unsightly, but they are proven deterrents to slug or snail attacks. The easiest are clear plastic bottles with the tops and bottoms cut off to form cylinders that can be placed around seedlings or small plants. Likewise, sheets of rigid plastic supported by bamboo stakes or PVC pipe can serve as walls, barring gastropods from otherwise vulnerable flowerbeds. Of course, it is important to ascertain that all slugs and snails have been removed from a plot *prior* to barrier installation, to avoid penning them in.

PUTTING A DASH OF SALT on a slug and then watching it melt—nearly every resident of Washington, Oregon, and northern California has tried this experiment at least once. Shame on us, though. The salt creates an ionic imbalance, which impels the animal to crawl out of its own slime and rapidly dehydrate. Because a slug's body surface contains numerous nerve endings, salting causes undue pain for the slug. In addition, too many applications will eventually make the soil toxic to all but a few salt-tolerant plants.

The best barriers are made of solid copper bands at least 3 inches (7.5 cm) wide. Because the electrons in copper molecules are only loosely bonded, any snail or slug that comes into contact with one of these bands will receive a slight electric shock. To increase the effectiveness of the copper, bend the upper edge of each band over and down, forming a flange.

Copper is expensive, so it becomes cost-effective to group slug-prone plants. You may wind up haunting scrap yards or hanging out at recycled building supply stores to find the best deals on pre-used copper sheeting. Several firms now sell adhesive-backed copper barrier tape, which works best on the sides of planter boxes or large glazed pots. Don't fret should your copper bands turn green with age, as their efficiency as electrified slug fences will not be diminished by such oxidation.

USE YOUR IMAGINATION

Nearly every devout gardener has invented a way to keep pulmonates in their place. One senior horticulturist with plenty of time on her hands actually builds small bridges of bran across partially buried coffee cans filled with soapy water. As a bridge crumbles under the modest weight of the gastropod crossing it, the animal is deposited in the inescapable suds.

Another folk invention involves putting slugs in a blender and repelling slugs by coating plant leaves with the resultant puree. Unfortunately, this home remedy requires daily applications and works only on slugs or snails that are the same as those in the glop. Furthermore, possible health risks from slug or snail parasites make the blender method more trouble than it is worth. And one would definitely want to acquire a second blender and set it aside solely for this purpose.

Sometimes the oddest remedies originate through scientific studies. While field-testing toxic agents to eliminate a non-native frog in Hawaii, a team of U.S. Department of Agriculture and U.S. Fish and Wildlife Service field researchers observed that a spray containing a one- to two-percent caffeine solution was sufficient for dispatching large slugs. Encouraged by initial results, they tried the two-percent solution on large slugs that had burrowed into the soil of potted plants. Wetting the soil with the caffeine solution, they waited and watched as the slugs left their burrows and began to writhe as if experiencing the coffee jitters. After 48 hours, all the slugs had left the soil and 92 percent of them were dead. The brew caused little damage to potted palms, orchids, or *Anthuriums*, but the caffeine caused the fronds of ferns, and leaves of bromeliads and lettuce plants to yellow.

These findings have inspired local gardeners to heap mounds of unused coffee grounds around their most valuable plants. While this tactic has been proven to quickly eliminate slugs and snails, it has also killed earthworms and has proven quite toxic to dogs. With coffee selling at a minimum of five dollars a pound, it is an expensive as well as environmentally damaging alternative.

A brief flirtation with *nematodes*—small parasitic worms that feed on and ultimately overpower slugs and snails—ended on a similar note. Although initially regarded as miracle worms, it soon became evident that the nematodes cannot discriminate between exotic pests and benign native species. For this reason alone, their use has been halted in the United States and Canada. The same goes for mollusk-munching decollate snails. Once regarded as the wunderkinds of the anti-snail movement, they lost their charm as word of their penchant for pulverizing native pulmonates spread.

DECOLLATE SNAIL

The tip of the decollate snail's shell is missing—the result of this snail's intentional efforts to grind it against a rock or other hard surface.

CHEMICAL WARFARE

Many commercial slug and snail baits are available today as pellets, meal, or emulsions. Most combine an attractant (usually apple meal or some other sweet-smelling base) with an active ingredient (most commonly the chemical compound metaldehyde) to poison whatever swallows the bait. Metaldehyde works by dehydrating its victims, so, theoretically speaking, in wet weather, slugs can rehydrate themselves, sloughing off a supposedly lethal dose.

Several slug bait manufacturers rely on carbamate compounds, originally developed as insecticides, to exterminate slugs. Others include a second poison, methiocarb (commercially sold as Mesurol).

A MAN HEARS A KNOCK at his front door and goes to answer it. He opens the door and there is no one there. He looks around. Nothing. He's about to go back inside when he notices a small snail on his front stoop. He shrugs, reaches down, picks up the snail and throws it into a vacant lot across the street.

Ten years later, he hears another knock at his door. Again, he finds no one there. He looks down and sees the snail. The snail looks up at him and says, "Now what was *that* all about?

Ingested metaldehyde can lead to nervous system damage or death in humans and other animals. The threshold for tolerance is related to size, making birds and small mammals especially vulnerable. Carbamates are even more toxic than metaldehyde to animals, including earthworms and other soil fauna. Because of its high toxicity to humans, methiocarb should not be used around food crops. If you decide to use baits containing any of these chemicals, use them judiciously. Usually the manufacturer's caveats will tell you more than you care to know. Here is a sample:

> Harmful if swallowed or absorbed through the skin. This pesticide may be fatal to children and dogs or other pets if eaten. Protect dogs from treated areas, since they may be attracted to this product when applied. This product is toxic to birds and other wildlife. Birds feeding on treated areas may be killed. Do not apply directly to water or contaminate water by cleaning of equipment or disposal of wastes.

Chemicals potentially pose one other problem—how to safely dispose of any chemical-laden corpses. While bodies collected from other means can be composted or flushed down the toilet, slugs and snails that have been poisoned should be buried away from your garden and any natural sources of water. This will allow most poisons to break down into harmless constituents over time, while preventing other land animals from becoming bioaccumulators.

"Nowadays, everyone is switching to Sluggo, Worry Free, or Escar-Go! slug bait," says Ciscoe Morris, Seattle's gardening guru. "Iron phosphate is the main ingredient in these products. It's relatively non-toxic and it works well. Hey, at the Northwest Flower and Garden Show, a woman selling one of the brands was eating it by the spoonful, to show how safe it is."

Oregon State University's Extension Service agents agree with Ciscoe's assessment. "After conducting trials with iron phosphate baits, [OSU entomologist Glen] Fisher and his colleagues have found that the less toxic iron phosphate containing slug baits are as effective as metaldehyde baits for controlling our common gray garden slug," Carol Savonen wrote in the Extension Service's *Gardening Hints.*

In summary, let's give our native pulmonates a break. Everyone belly up to the salad bar and raise your steins of Kingsbury Malt Beverage in a toast to these silent toilers of our forests, fens, and fields. At the same time, let's become the bouncers at the bar, giving non-native land snails and slugs the boot. Let's not put any other forms of wildlife, including ourselves and our neighbors, needlessly at risk from the misuse (and overuse) of molluscicides. And let's proceed slowly, taking time to get to know, if not live, a "Life in the Very Slow Lane."

A Gloomy Future for Land Gastropods?

Slugs and snails that withstand our traps, poisons, and introduced predators may still be doomed by forces of nature far beyond their control. Rising sea levels and shifts in seasonal weather patterns, both wrought by climate change, could overcome these animals in many parts of the world. Unable to survive under more physiologically taxing conditions, hundreds and possibly thousands of pulmonate species could soon join their relatives from the Cretaceous-Tertiary period on the already lengthy list of extinct mollusk species.

The pace of their extinction has been accelerated by the fast and loose lifestyles of our species. The conversion of historic woodlands to rural and suburban estates has put remarkable pressure on native slugs and snails, most of which have fairly inflexible food and habitat needs that, in many instances, can only be met by intact old-growth forests. Having lost their homes, many populations of wild snails are disappearing from the West.

It's impossible to predict what the full effects of urbanization will be on our native gastropod fauna. Data from other parts of the world tends to indicate that whatever they are, it won't be for the general good. In Switzerland, for example, one field study revealed that the corpse snail, *Arianta arbuston*, had vanished from more than half of its habitual haunts. The reason for the corpse snail's sudden demise? Increased air temperatures stemming from heat-absorbent surfaces surrounding the city of Basel.

The phenomenon known as acid rain—rain, snow, fog, sleet, and hail exhibiting high levels of nitric and sulfuric acids— is also drastically altering the land slugs' and snails' surroundings for the worse. Sources of acid rain are linked to human activities, in particular the burning of fossil fuels by coal-fueled power plants and factories, and the operation of petroleum-powered ocean freighters and automobiles. When sulfur dioxide and nitrogen oxide gases from these sources are released into the atmosphere, they react with water, oxygen, and other substances to form acidic solutions that fall to earth and ultimately, seep into the soil. Over time, the increased acidity robs the soil of essential nutrients and, by damaging root systems, weakens trees and shrubs.

By decreasing the levels of calcium in soil, acid rain is rendering some habitats inhospitable to land snails. Studies conducted in the Buunderkamp forest, west of the Dutch city of Arnhem, showed that, where soils were already poor, acid rain has caused land snail abundance to plummet. Such declines make it impossible for snail-eating songbirds such as the great tit (*Parus major*) to meet their dietary requirement for calcium—an essential mineral for making thick, unbreakable eggshells. Without snails to eat, the songbirds are laying defective eggs, incapable of hatching.

But I would like to conclude this book with some good news. In the Czech Republic, malacologists have discovered that the ruins of medieval castles are serving as sanctuaries for habitat-deprived snails and slugs. A sweep of 114 Czech castles yielded 110 species of gastropod mollusks—or 70 percent of the terrestrial slug and snail species living within the nation's borders. Of these species, 20 percent were ranked as critically endangered (one species), endangered (seven species), or vulnerable (sixteen species) on the International Union of Conservation of Nature's Red List for the Czech Republic.

Snail upon the wall,
Have you got at all
Anything to tell
About your shell?

Only this, my child—
When the wind is wild,
Or when the sun is hot,
It's all I've got.

—JOHN DRINKWATER,
Snail

For Additional Reading

Abott, R. Tucker. *A Compendium of Landshells: A Color Guide to more than 2,000 of the World's Terrestrial Shells,* Melbourne, FL: American Malacologists, Inc., 1989.

Forsyth, Robert G. *Land Snails of British Columbia,* Victoria, BC: Royal British Columbia Museum, 2004.

Harper, Alice Bryant. *Banana Slug: A Close Look at a Giant Forest Slug of Western North America,* Aptos, CA: Bay Leaves Press, 1988.

Kozloff, Eugene. *Plants and Animals of the Pacific Northwest,* Seattle, WA: University of Washington Press, 1976.

Roth, Barry, and Patricia S. Sadeghian. *Checklist of the Land Snails and Slugs of California,* Santa Barbara, CA: Santa Barbara Museum of Natural History, 2006.

Solem, Alan. *The Shell Makers: Introducing the Mollusks,* New York: John Wiley & Sons, 1974.

About the Author

David George Gordon is the award-winning author of nineteen books on topics ranging from horses, gray whales, and bald eagles to cockroaches, spiders, and geoduck clams. He has given presentations at the Smithsonian Institution, American Museum of Natural History, San Diego Zoo, and other prestigious venues in the United States and overseas. When not on the trail of slugs and snails, Gordon serves as the science writer for Washington Sea Grant, a NOAA program headquartered at the University of Washington. He lives in Seattle.